The
CHRIST
of
Easter

Readings for the Season of Resurrection

The
CHRIST
of
Easter

CALVIN MILLER

B&H
PUBLISHING GROUP
Nashville, Tennessee

To Barbara

Introduction

This book is a 48-day reader designed to look at the crucifixion and exaltation of Christ. It begins with Shrove Tuesday, the eve of the six-week journey most Christians honor as the pre-Easter season.

It is my fondest hope that you, my reader, will not hurry this volume by reading it too quickly. It is written to be a one-day-at-a-time book, the content of which is to be set down in the midst of the reader's own pilgrimage of prayer and introspection. Its intention is to ready your soul for the whole Easter event, by allowing you to spend your soul in an attempt to appreciate the price Christ paid to redeem you. If you meet your Savior and offer him your praise at this book's ending, I will be more than compensated for my work.

So come let us journey toward his victory and claim it— one day at a time—for our own. For so it is.

The Author

47 Days Until Easter

The father told his slaves, "Quick! Bring out the best robe and put it on him; put a ring on his finger and sandals on his feet. Then bring the fattened calf and slaughter it, and let's celebrate with a feast, because this son of mine was dead and is alive again; he was lost and is found!" So they began to celebrate. (Luke 15:22–24)

Have you ever noticed how brokenness and joy often come into our lives together? How the despair over our sin is quickly swallowed up in the smile of Christ's forgiveness? Like the prodigal son, we too discover that beyond the overwhelming sorrow of our repentance comes the cake and ice cream, the party caps and whistles of God's grace. Our confession starts the party. The recapturing of our discarded joy sets the angels dancing, filling heaven with holy revelry, rejoicing, and merry-making.

This is why we should unashamedly begin our Easter experience with Shrove Tuesday—Fat Tuesday, as it is more commonly called. On this Tuesday we discover again that God is a

Father who enjoys seeing his children experience life and happiness, warmth and family.

Do some abuse this annual dive into gluttonous unrestraint? Yes. But we should not despise their indulgence as though all enjoyment is bad for the soul. Joy and Jesus should never find themselves pages apart in our dictionaries.

Shrove Tuesday is here to remind us—and amaze us—that the season of Easter is both prefaced and climaxed with celebrations. In fact, Jesus taught that heaven is a constant party, for the angels daily enroll the names of those who have confessed their sins and joined the kingdom of God.

And in those churches where evangelism is customary, "new saints" are the daily expectation. These churches know why the angels continually sing. For the joy of heaven touches earth whenever honest prodigals confess their sins and enter the wide embrace of God. In such churches it is always Easter. There Christ daily works his life-changing wonder.

Shrove Tuesday calls us to a universal truth: God never wraps his arms around a weeping prodigal without

How glorious to find our soiled clothes replaced by rings and robes.

yelling to the starry court, "This—my child—was dead and is alive again; this one who was lost has been found.

"It's party time!"

Prayer

Lord, have I forgotten that tears are made for laughing as well as for crying, and that prodigals reborn set all of heaven singing? This Easter season, may I remember again your pain and sacrifice. May my rightful anguish over my participation in Christ's dying be dissolved in the joy of his resurrection.

For additional Bible reading: Isaiah 61:10–11

46 Days until Easter

Now a man was sick, Lazarus, from Bethany, the village of Mary and her sister Martha. . . . So the sisters sent a message to [Jesus]: "Lord, the one You love is sick." When Jesus heard it, He said, "This sickness will not end in death, but is for the glory of God, so that the Son of God may be glorified through it." (John 11:1, 3–4)

Today is Ash Wednesday—a solemn reminder that we are upon this earth for only a very short time. For as Longfellow reminds us, "'Dust thou art, to dust returnest,' was not spoken of the soul." Our days are relatively few, our hurried Easters are always piling up behind us. And yet we still have so many sins to conquer. So many failures yet to amend. So many times when the love of our dying Christ fails to rouse us to grateful obedience.

In the passage above, Lazarus is sick. Be it cancer or the common cold, sickness is never pleasant. But there is a wasting sickness in the human heart that causes it to grow stony. Such hardness smothers the stirring of spiritual desire. Both physical and spiritual sicknesses can leave us lonely, in need of someone to bring the healing balm of help and encouragement.

Yet sometimes, painful as it is, sickness is what we need most. We need to face the encroaching spectre of our future death to jar us from our hypnotic presumptions. The facing of our "temporariness" awakes us to our dependence on that life we find only in Jesus.

So Christ came to Lazarus, to heal him from something much more ominous than sickness: he came to rescue him from death. Jesus knew what Lazarus could not have guessed—that Lazarus was going to die, but only temporarily. Jesus knew that Lazarus would come back from the dead. And the furor that erupted around his resurrection would catapult Jesus to the very center of an uproar during the last turbulent weeks of his life.

> God's glory often lives in the deepest recesses of our pain.

What is before you on this Ash Wednesday? Is it the pain of your own sin? The ache of some ongoing trial? Does it look like the events in your near future are gathered about you like a covey of demons threatening to wipe out your happiness?

Remember what Jesus said of Lazarus' sickness. Your circumstances become the very occasion that God wants to use to glorify himself. Our small affairs and gut-wrenching problems are often just potential points of praise. Ash Wednesday prefaces the Easter season with the suggestion that we are temporary. Easter concludes the season with a reminder that "temporary" is a word missing from God's vocabulary.

Prayer

Lord, help me to face every storm—even the blinding cloud of my own sinfulness—with the resolution that you are present in the thunder and the roaring, the tossing and the turning. Come craft Christlikeness from my unreliable heart. Take my mortality and dress it in immortality.

For additional Bible reading: Psalm 34:17–19

45 Days Until Easter

Jesus then told them painly, "Lazarus has died. I'm glad for you that I wasn't there, so that you may believe. But let's go to him." Then Thomas (called "Twin") said to his fellow disciples, "Let's go so that we may die with Him."
(John 11:14–16)

Lazarus was dead. Jerusalem was looming large as a city of death and terror where Jesus' disciples must enter at their own risk. Jesus knew this would be his final visit to the city. He knew he was going there to die. But he also knew that God was about to keep his appointment with human redemption.

The disciples understood that to know the price of their discipleship and refuse to pay would have been disloyal. So all of them—at this time, at least—took a stand to follow Jesus, regardless of the cost.

Thomas spoke openly of the danger of this trip. He seemed to know that Calvary is not something Jesus did *for* us so much as it is something he does *with* us. Thomas wisely feared.

Crosses cost. Each of us must take up our cross and follow him, knowing that the cross invites us to a fellowship of suffering.

But still, the gravity of Jesus' decision must have rested more heavily on Christ than on Thomas or any of the others. For what Christ knew, they only suspected. He knew the days of his young life were winding down to the appointment he must keep. He knew he was the incarnate Son of God. He knew the price he would pay: his life. He also knew the glorious end of the whole drama would be his resurrection. Now just weeks before he died, Lazarus was dead.

> Discipleship at its heart is a covenant of following, no matter what.

Dead? Yes, but not for long. What Christ the Savior had in mind would astound the city of Jerusalem. He was about to give the world a close-up look at his power over life and death. Lazarus would live again.

Therefore, all of Jerusalem would soon tremble under the impact of one overwhelming new idea:

Death is not forever.

Indeed, Lazarus was not so dead as he appeared.

Prayer

Lord, as Lazarus was your friend, may my friendship yield my own confidence in your power of resurrection. Further, I want to thank you that I too will one day find my own tomb torn apart, so that all Lazarus knew in resurrection, I too shall some day know in my triumph over death. May I be willing to follow you with glorious abandon, knowing that nothing is more important than being counted among your friends.

For additional Bible reading: Hebrews 12:1–3

"Your brother will rise again," Jesus told her.
Martha said, "I know that he will rise again in
the resurrection at the last day." Jesus said to her,
"I am the resurrection and the life. The one who
believes in Me, even if he dies, will live. Everyone
who lives and believes in Me will never die—ever."
(John 11:23–26)

Jesus' greatest teachings often came in short syllables. Here he set two words against all dying—*resurrection* and *life*. He reminded us that every time we stand beside an open grave and bid good-bye to a loved one, we participate in a grieving illusion. No Christian grave is eternal.

Often when Jesus spoke, he presented a definition in process. This is one of those occasions. Martha would require six more weeks to fully appreciate what Jesus was saying, much as we are spending these six weeks pondering the depths of Easter's phrases and events. Yes, Lazarus was about to break out of his shallow, impermanent grave. But Martha's understanding of what Jesus was saying would only be partially apparent when her brother returned to life. The fullest definition of all Jesus was saying would make no sense until he himself came out of the tomb.

These two resurrections—Jesus' and Lazarus's—are quite a bit different:

❖ Lazarus's coming back to life represented only a regaining of his pulse and respiration. When Jesus came back to life, he somehow had outgrown his dependency on oxygen.

❖ Lazarus would come back to life only to face another dying later. Jesus returned forever free of all dying.

❖ Lazarus's return to life was only a short reprieve, a biological postponement. Jesus' resurrection was truly an everlasting triumph over death.

In some ways, Lazarus's resurrection was a kind of theological overture to the symphony of Easter. In other ways it was like a report from behind the high gates of death, over which none could see and which all believed could not be opened. Yet Jesus cried, "Lazarus, come forth," and the gates were splintered by the gales of an invisible life force.

> The dead cannot sleep when Christ has ordered them awake.

We cannot trivialize this miracle even by setting it alongside Easter. Lazarus's resurrection was a bold reversal, strong enough to declare that in all matters of death and dying, God always gets the last word.

Prayer

Lord, the grim date and the black wreath are deceptions sent to gnaw at faith. Help us to see that life—not death—is real. Help us to keep Lazarus in our minds, so that we can really understand what you have in store for us. We want your words of resurrection and life to define the "foreverness" that marks our future.

For additional Bible reading: 1 John 5:11–13

43 Days Until Easter

When Jesus saw [Mary] crying, and the Jews who had come with her crying, He was angry in His spirit and deeply moved. "Where have you put him?" He asked. "Lord," they told Him, "come and see." Jesus wept. (John 11:33–35)

What made Jesus weep? Could it have been human faithlessness? Mary and Martha sorrowed so hopelessly in his presence. Here was Jesus, God's Son, for whom any miracle was possible, yet these women of Bethany sorrowed as if nothing could be done. Here was human desperation standing next to resurrection power.

Could it be that Jesus still weeps when we refuse to trust the God who is sovereign over all heartache?

What else made Jesus weep? Could it have been their slowness to understand that to be absent from the body is to be present with the Lord? Jesus was close—hauntingly close—to his own death. He knew that Lazarus was in a much better world than the one Mary and Martha wished him to be back in. Now he must bring Lazarus—perhaps kicking and screaming—back to the world at hand.

> **For the Christian, weeping is seasonal, joy eternal.**

What else made Jesus weep? Could it have been sheer grief? Jesus loved Lazarus as much as he despised death. He grieved Lazarus's passing. This is the Christ who never lets human sorrow exist alone. This is the Christ about whom the prophet said, "Surely he hath borne our griefs and carried our sorrows."

Jesus wept because he was part of our human condition. He was made in all ways like we are. Jesus did not take up our condition free of tear ducts. He wept because we all weep. He cried, and his tears demonstrated his humanity.

Such a weeping Christ is worthy of our full acceptance, worthy of our worship.

Prayer

Lord, thank you for weeping with Mary and Martha. It helps me to remember how much you despise death and how much I depend on your tears when I must face my own seasons of grief. My joy is made full when I remember heaven is capable of tears.

For additional Bible reading: Hebrews 4:14–16

He took the Twelve aside and told them, "Listen! We are going up to Jerusalem. Everything that is written through the prophets about the Son of Man will be accomplished. For He will be handed over to the Gentiles, and He will be mocked, insulted, spit on; and after they flog Him, they will kill Him, and He will rise on the third day." They understood none of these things. This saying was hidden from them, and they did not grasp what was said. Luke 18:31–33

Jesus brought his disciples to the planning tables of God, and still they remained obtuse. Pity these disciples, but remember this: they were simply so human—so much like us—that their little minds could not wrangle with the huge redemptive dreams of God. En route to the cross, Jesus tried to tell them what he wished them to understand: he would have to die to finish the plan of God.

What must Jesus' mood have been when they failed to understand him? It cannot have been utter despair. Yet he must have seen in their blank expressions the chilling reminder that his work of redeeming the sons and daughters of the world would be a lonely and fearful undertaking.

Not only would his *dying* be lonely, but also his *living*. He knew he must continue on toward Calvary, carrying a vision so large that his twelve friends could not imagine the weight of it.

From this moment on, he must endure more sorrow than even his best friends could possibly understand. How could he live at all carrying what he did? He knew that when all other human support began to dwindle around him, God would draw very close to him with a rapport only the Father and Son could experience. Count the times that Jesus used the word "Father" in the

> Those who are content with pleasing others have ceased being Christian and are merely humanitarian.

last six weeks of his life, and you will see how his soul fed on the iron grip of God's love.

Even on the cross we see this glorious rapport. We hear the Father's earlier words, cried once again over the river Jordan: "This is my beloved Son, in whom I am well pleased."

The desperate and lonely work of the cross would be accomplished by a Son who would give his last drop of blood to please his Father—a Father who treasured his Son's devotion . . . and understood.

Prayer

Lord, I want to please you just as you sought to please your Father. It is not enough that I go to church or perform small religious acts. Unless I gain your smile, carrying my own cross will bring me little pleasure. In this way only will I measure the reason for my life.

For additional Bible reading: Psalm 62:5–8

41 Days Until Easter

James and John, the sons of Zebedee, approached Him and said, "Teacher, we want You to do something for us if we ask You." "What do you want Me to do for you?" He asked them. "Grant us," they answered Him, "that we may sit at Your right and at Your left in Your glory." (Mark 10:35–37)

The lust for power is a universal, longstanding appetite. We know that in our day, many long for control and influence within the church. But even before the cross, the true colors of two of Jesus' disciples had already begun seeing the kingdom of God as a political arena of position and leverage. James and John brazenly said to Jesus, "We want a special place in your kingdom, Lord. We want authority, recognition . . . power."

We are intrigued not just because James and John *wanted* power (after all, just about everyone wants that). What *is* intriguing is that James and John actually could have thought Jesus would grant it to them.

In Matthew 20:21, the Gospel writer tells us that it was the *mother* of James and John who made this elitist request. Behind James and John's desire for power was a pushy mom. Perhaps these aspiring young men wanted to be the "vice presidents" of Jesus' kingdom because they felt this would make their mother proud of them.

But let us not lay all the blame on their mother. It is a real possibility that James and John wanted their special friendship to be of some "useful" advantage to them in the kingdom of God. Still, it was sheer folly to press this. Jesus had no special friends, and granting people the right to govern others was never his agenda. Jesus wants no one to think of his kingdom as a place for political maneuvering. We do not accept Christ merely to control others. The only reason we should want to be close to Jesus is to know the sheer pleasure of his companionship.

Some still go to church to be seen by "the right people," so that they may in time become one of "the right people" themselves. But healthy Christians go to church to be united with

> For those in Christ, the longing for prestige is the parent of treachery.

Christ, to place their ambitions at the foot of the cross. Straight-thinking disciples know that power-lust is born from egotisms unyet cleansed.

Prayer

Easter is coming, Lord, and with it the reminder that you, who already possessed your rightful place as King, abandoned your realm to accept the limitations of ours. It is difficult not to crave power in this competitive world; but please, Lord, help me crave the pleasure of your company instead. Ruling over others is far less significant than loving my life in your presence.

For additional Bible reading: Nehemiah 5:14–19

40 Days Until Easter

"When the Son of Man sits on His glorious throne, you who have followed Me will also sit on 12 thrones, judging the 12 tribes of Israel. And everyone who has left houses, brothers or sisters, father or mother, children, or fields because of My name will receive 100 times more and will inherit eternal life. But many who are first will be last, and the last first." (Matthew 19:28–30)

Who will be the most prominent people in heaven? List your top ten. We generally list church leaders and evangelists, popes and council people as holding heaven's chief seats. But how much chance is there that these will be the most prominent ones? Is it possible that those who have achieved religious prominence in this world will find their heavenly glory eclipsed by devout chambermaids and praying cobblers?

The pecking order of heaven is not based on earthly triumphs. Heaven will measure our achievements by how we've lived up to the level of our gifts. God wants us to be ardent in pursuing service and private adoration. In heaven we shall be measured only against the level of our abilities.

Heaven's pecking order contains a wonderful glory: God will never require of us anything he has not equipped us to achieve. But to achieve heaven as a place of power must never concern us. What genuine believer ever wanted to go to heaven just to gain power? There is only one real motive in heaven: a lover's desire to be united with Christ.

Perhaps this craving itself designates all who would be first. Those who love Christ the most on earth will stand closest in eternity to the object of their love.

Should we not, then, lose ourselves in worship this Easter? Will this longing not compel us to be ministers among those he died to save? In short, all things wonderful begin in our adoration of Christ.

We often hear that the world has yet to see what a soul entirely devoted to Christ might accomplish. Only his supreme love could motivate such a servant. Such driving ardor will never hunger to rule in heaven. It will only glory in its coming union with Christ.

The humble rarely see those strengths that so endear them to God.

Prayer

Lord, I care not about position in heaven. Let all those bent on having power rule there as they may. Give me only a small place close enough to see your face. Your face alone defines the boundaries of all that golden land. If you withhold your presence from all that we call heaven, the place itself dissolves and has no point.

For additional Bible reading: 1 Peter 5:1–6

> *Mary took a pound of fragrant oil—pure and expensive*
> *nard—anointed Jesus' feet, and wiped His feet with her*
> *hair. So the house was filled with the fragrance of the oil.*
> *Then one of His disciples, Judas Iscariot (who was about*
> *to betray Him), said, "Why wasn't this fragrant oil sold*
> *for three hundred denarii and given to the poor?"*
> *(John 12:3–5)*

Frugality or extravagance: which does God favor? Which of these attitudes toward the material world does Jesus have?

Look at Jesus himself. He was not a wealthy person, and yet he seems to have skimmed his joy from the top of life. He knew how to celebrate. He attended social events so frequently he was called a "glutton" and a "winebibber." These unkind slurs against his reputation confirm his love of parties. There is certainly no sin in this, but it does raise the question: "How could Jesus go to so many parties when he came on such a serious mission of redemption?"

When Mary dumped her costly perfume on the feet of Jesus, this question was answered. Stewardship is important, but not so all-important that the disciples of Christ are to become stingy in their celebrations of his outrageous grace. Mary's gift was so extravagant that it serves to remind us of the lavish abundance of God.

Consider a thousand acres of wildflowers, and ask yourself how frugal God is. Consider the myriads of life forms, hidden in the dark heart of unseen seas. Why so large and varied a biological world? Is not God lavish in how he frames the universe?

Now think of how God saves, how freely the blood of Christ, like a large and lavish river, completely deluges us in joyous forgiveness. No one was ever rescued from sin by stingy applications of the blood of Christ.

Critics are stingy spenders, avoiding the lavish sprees of shoppers ruled by love.

So Mary, whom God had abundantly forgiven, came to Jesus. She dared not dab a bit of spikenard here and there on Jesus. She did not receive his grace that way; she would not give that way. She dumped the sweetness, worth at least ten thousand dollars in today's currency, on the object of her adoration. Judas said it was a waste of money. But Jesus knew better. Lavish is as lavish does.

Prayer

Lord, abundance is your very nature. If I give by ledger and carefully count the coins, I sin against a God who despises penny-pinching giving. O God, lavishly you love. May any stinginess, therefore, never be welcome in my life. May I give as you give.

For additional Bible reading: 2 Corinthians 9:6–8

38 Days Until Easter

Six days before the Passover, Jesus came to Bethany where Lazarus was, whom Jesus had raised from the dead. So they gave a dinner for him there; Martha was serving them, and Lazarus was one of those reclining at the table with Him. . . . Then a large crowd of the Jews learned that He was there. They came not only because of Jesus, but also to see Lazarus whom He had raised from the dead. (John 12:1–2, 9)

Bethany was but a little place, yet it held a spectacle that was hard to shout down. There went the doubters to watch a once-dead man eat. Lazarus may have been the first person in history to attend his own funeral dinner. It's enough to make the blood run cold.

But then, look! Jesus sat eating right beside him. Was the phenomenon containable? Perhaps scores of villagers even crowded about the house to peek in and have a look at Lazarus—back from the dead and eating once again.

The Pharisees attending this "resurrection sideshow" realized the wonder and yet did not retreat before it. They realized that if Jesus was going to be stopped, they needed to kill both Jesus and Lazarus. It would do little good to kill Jesus and leave Lazarus alive. Someone who was formerly dead would always stand as proof that Jesus—who had raised him—was someone of note.

Perhaps what is most remarkable about this highly observed dinner is that the Pharisees never saw the wonder of it. They were out to kill Jesus' reputation, even if they had to kill Jesus to do it. They could no longer widen their vision to see the wonder of all they wanted to do away with. "Get Jesus!" was so much their agenda that they could no longer open their hearts to the sheer glory of watching a former dead man eating.

> To behold the Christ should call to life the wonder and worship lying dead within us.

So much for the Pharisees. How about you?

❖ Do you trip into church several times a month to do religious service of one kind or another?

❖ Did you hear that a child has just received Christ as Savior? You ought to stop and rejoice and congratulate, but you've no time to encounter wonder. You have your own separate, smaller religious agendas to carry out.

❖ Do you, in keeping your nose to the religious grindstone, say, "No time for wonder! Out of my way with all things glorious. I must attend to the religious—I have no time for the vital."

Be careful. With such preoccupation the Pharisees lost the wonder of Jesus' mighty acts . . . and forged a crucifixion.

Prayer

Lord, when did I go from vital to busy? When did I trade the wonder of following Jesus for the business of playing church? Give me back my former love. Restore unto me the joy of your salvation.

For additional Bible reading: Psalm 111:2–9

3 7 Days Until Easter

When they approached Jerusalem and came to Bethphage at the Mount of Olives, Jesus then sent two disciples, telling them, "Go into the village ahead of you. At once you will find a donkey tied there, and a colt with her. Untie them and bring them to Me. If anyone says anything to you, you should say that the Lord needs them, and immediately he will send them." (Matthew 21:1–3)

Why own what you can borrow? At the mere suggestion of this, our modern ears are dumbfounded. That's just not the way we do it anymore.

Perhaps if Jesus had been a modern preacher, he might have made an impassioned plea for money to buy his own triumphal entry donkey. We can almost hear his rhetoric: "Step, right up! We must raise a hundred denarii to buy this strong, young, triumphal-entry donkey. Cash, checks, or money orders are welcome. Be a part of this world-changing event—the triumphal entry. If your pledge is large enough, this marvelous beast can even be *named* after you!"

But Jesus was not out to own a donkey. The kingdom could

be served best, in fact, if Jesus owned nothing. So he only *borrowed* the donkey:

❖ After all, he just needed it for a short ride.

❖ He merely wanted it as a means of making a statement.

❖ He was only going to use it as a way of declaring that the Messiah was on earth.

❖ He required it in order to fulfill the words of Zechariah 9:9. After that, the prophecy would be fulfilled and the donkey could be returned to its owner.

Strangely, the owner seemed quite congenial in loaning it to him. Is it not remarkable that he made no requirement to be recognized as the donor? He marked no little plaque which read, "Donkey courtesy of . . ." No, the Master had need of a donkey, and this unnamed man who was privy to Jesus' right to lordship said, "Here, take the donkey. Go and make the prophet Zechariah look good."

Thus, in this one little passage of Scripture, Jesus teaches us how to use possessions without being possessed by them, and an unknown donkey owner is seen participating in the plan of the

> Better a monarch on a donkey than a tyrant on a steed.

ages. His example challenges us to always be open to the possibilities of God.

Something we own even now may be of use to Jesus. Let us be swift and generous in the surrender of all our gifts to him.

Prayer

Lord, as I see you approaching the cross, I am amazed at your continual willingness to sacrifice, to be obedient, to remain content. Oh, how I wish to be! What is it that I have not yet surrendered? Help me to freely give it. Let your single enticement—"The Master has need of it"—lead me to respond instantly to your request. May nothing else need be said.

For additional Bible reading: 1 Timothy 6:17–19

36 Days Until Easter

On the first day of Unleavened Bread, when they sacrifice the Passover lamb, His disciples asked Him, "Where do you want us to go and prepare the Passover so You may eat it?" So He sent two of His disciples and told them, "Go into the city, and a man carrying a water jug will meet you. Follow him. Wherever he enters, tell the owner of the house, 'The Teacher says, "Where is the guest room for Me to eat the Passover with My disciples?" (Mark 14:12–14)

Do you know how the disciples knew which man to look for, carrying which water pot, on which Jerusalem street? Put yourself back in Jesus' world. Any man carrying a water pot would stand out, for men in those days rarely carried water. *Women* carried the water pots. So a male carrying a water pot would be quite easy to spot.

Some have suggested that this unnamed water carrier was John Mark. If true, the Last Supper may have been celebrated in Mark's more palatial home. We cannot know this for sure. But we do know the disciples seemed not to know who the man was—even if Jesus did—for they did indeed follow the man, apparently in ignorance, until they had fulfilled the will of Christ.

In spite of his anonymity, this man carrying a water pot became a key player in the final events of Christ's life. In this way the story of the water pot is much like the tale of the borrowed donkey in yesterday's reading—an earthly "unknown" becoming eternally unforgettable.

Water carriers do count with God. The gospel of grace is largely the stories of water boys and fallen women. In short, the gospel is the tale of little people surprised to find themselves engulfed in the great plan of God. Like this unsuspecting water carrier, they found themselves center-stage in God's unfolding drama of redemption.

What is the irresistible nature of this grace? This water carrier seemed not to be out looking for God when he stumbled upon Jesus' disciples and was swallowed whole by the purposes of God. No matter. God is there in a thousand ways throwing up barriers and saying, "Stop where you are! You thought you were going out to perform some menial, minor task. En route to

> No task to which the Father has called you is insignificant.

serve this trivia, you fell into my immensity. Welcome to the majesty of my kingdom. Your life is suddenly bigger than it ever would have been if you had not been interrupted by God's demanding reality."

Prayer

Lord, I remember when my life was consumed by eating from little menus, running small errands, and keeping small appointments. Were it not for your love, were it not for your reaching into my one-dimensional world—were it not for Easter—I might still be lost in my trivial pursuits. Thank you, Lord, for engulfing me in the gigantic purposes of your grace.

For additional Bible reading: Isaiah 44:21–23

35 Days Until Easter

After throwing their robes on the donkey, they helped Jesus get on it. As He was going along, they were spreading their robes on the road. Now He came near the path down the Mount of Olives, and the whole crowd of the disciples began to praise God joyfully with a loud voice for all the miracles. (Luke 19: 35–37)

Palm Sunday is still a full four weeks away. But let us visit it ahead of time, for it has lessons to teach before we arrive. The mind's eye is a way for us to prepare, to feel every heartbeat of Christ as he approaches his cross.

The Palm Sunday event is unquestionably the last hurrah of the earthly Christ.

Four days beyond the mass pageantry, Jesus was in Gethsemane, and five days later he was on the cross. So we come face-to-face with the fickle human spirit as we ask, "How could Jesus be both celebrated and condemned within a five-day period?"

> Even when curses rear their heads, love often abandons its creed.

His mass acceptance and denial were challengingly close together.

We must not assume that Jesus was so deluded by his Palm Sunday acclaim that the condemnation of Good Friday surprised him. Never did Jesus look around, stunned, as if to say, "Father, I'm sure surprised at how fast my celebration turned into crucifixion." Jesus knew the treacherous nature of humankind. In our fallen world it is possible to be a hero on Sunday and crucified the following Friday.

Christ managed to achieve something we find so difficult to master in our own lives—trusting others enough to freely serve them, yet not committing ourselves to their unstable sense of allegiance. For example, Jesus loved Judas as much as he loved the other disciples, but he was not shattered when Judas betrayed him. Because he understood the treachery of human nature, he loved Judas anyway.

He does the same with us. How often we have disappointed Christ, yet he is never destroyed by our momentary betrayals. Betrayal is human, but then humanity was his business.

Palm Sunday is evidence that we are to serve our friends and even to receive their accolades. We must always remember, however, that only God is perfect. Friends can disappoint us. But if we love like Christ, we must keep on loving them even as they disappoint us.

Prayer

Lord, knowing how fickle I am in loving you, help me not to be debilitated when my own friends begin to betray me. Loving the unlovely has always been your kind of love. Help me to remember that such love is really grace simply wearing an earthier garment.

For additional Bible reading: John 2:23–25

When the chief priests and the scribes saw the wonders that He did, and the children in the temple complex cheering, "Hosanna to the Son of David!" they were indignant and said to Him, "Do You hear what these children are saying?" "Yes," Jesus told them. "Have you never read: 'From the mouths of children and nursing infants You have prepared praise'?" (Matthew 21:15–16)

Theologians are rarely cheerleaders. They so often wear themselves out with heavy ideas that they lose the art of joy. Theologians make a living thinking about God. They sometimes—sooner or later—become God's elitists. They are full of answers and insight but all too often void of praise. Yet Palm Sunday proves one point: when the religious elite refuse to praise God, he knows he can always turn to those whose praise is more automatic.

Both children and theologians were part of the Palm Sunday throng. One can only imagine that the theologians had spent a very hard morning working through the importance of old

Hebrew word roots. Their scholarship was rigorous, and it left them so distracted, they never saw the Son of God when he entered the city. The children, well . . . they were quite another matter. They loved Jesus and were so glad to see him coming into Jerusalem, they began shouting their uninhibited praises.

"Why are you children so boisterous?" we can imagine the Pharisees asking.

"Jesus is coming—he loves us kids, you know?"

"Well, pipe down. He's just an ordinary man. He's not the Son of David. We'll have no more praise of this non-Messiah!"

But the children just kept praising him anyway, so the Pharisees decided to take their complaint up with Jesus in person. They told him that the children were not only loud and offensive; they were being outright blasphemous. Jesus reminded them of an old Scripture that said children and infants would be the very ones who would praise the Messiah.

Palm Sunday was a glum day for theology. For certain kinds of scholars, nothing is worse than a field rabbi quoting Scripture to a theologian.

> Let the child you used to be praise him, and the adult you have become will be refreshed.

The Pharisees left, however—grumping their way back to their Hebrew word roots.

Yet the children sang on. Children always sing better than theologians, and songs hang in the air longer than theology. We can only wonder who felt better that day—the children or the theologians. Praise is better medicine than mere insight.

Prayer

Lord, help me to feel deep within my heart the praises that I offer you. Help me to study to become an informed believer, yes, but never let my scholarship steal the joy of our friendship. Keep me at the business of praise. It may not help me change my world, but it will keep my world from changing me.

For additional Bible reading: Psalm 8:1–9

33 Days Until Easter

Now my soul is troubled. What should I say—'Father, save Me from this hour'? But that is why I came to this hour. Father, glorify Your name!" Then a voice came from heaven: "I have glorified it, and I will glorify it again!"
(John 12:27–28)

Did your father want to be proud of you?

How did you reward his desire?

Did you act in ways designed to please him?

How far were you willing to go in the matter?

Wrestling with these questions will enable you to better understand the heart of God.

Cast your eye toward the cross. Do you see him? Jesus? Look! He faces the cross. Of course, he was troubled. Who at thirty-three years of age wants to die? Who in the prime of life wants to consider the horror of a torturous execution?

Yet Jesus never allowed his troubles to plunge him into the depths of despair, for he was preoccupied with a love affair he could not surrender. He never allowed his despair to cause him to forget why he came. People die with purpose when they have clearly marked the reason they were given life. Jesus existed to do the will of God. Since doing what his Father wanted would bring pleasure to the both of them, Christ was thus occupied with the pleasure of God.

Jesus served this single passion: to glorify God—to live to serve him, to please him. He faced every moral decision at every juncture of his life with only one concern: how will my decision affect my Father?

Seeing that such a passion owned Christ, how can we become Christlike? We must seek what he sought. Our chief duty is to glorify God and to enjoy him forever. Think of how your world would change if in every moment of decision, you did only those things that you knew would bring glory to the Son of God. In such a life there would be power!

In such a life there would also be simplicity. To want only one thing is to achieve purity of heart. To want only one thing puts to silence the competition of your

There is but one sweet phrase on my soul's shelf. It is this: "Father, glorify yourself."

inner appetites. To want only one thing silences the quarrel of trying to serve both Jesus and your own need for power.

Glorify God! Let this be your reason to live! You will then love God. And the simplicity of loving him so singularly will help you to discover and love yourself as well.

Prayer

Lord, glorify yourself through me. May I exalt you in every moment of decision. May my exaltation of you be my reason for being. I then shall be a person with clear purposes, and you will be able to use me in ways that you never could while I was too central in my own mind.

For additional Bible reading: 1 Peter 3:13–15

32 Days Until Easter

"He told his slaves, 'The banquet is ready, but those who were invited were not worthy. Therefore go to where the roads exit the city and invite everyone you find to the banquet.' So those slaves went out on the roads and gathered everyone they found, both evil and good. The wedding banquet was filled with guests. But when the king came in to view the guests, he saw a man there who was not dressed for a wedding." (Matthew 22:8–11)

Even during the final weeks of his life, Jesus continued to tell his stories of life and divine love. Had he preached only storyless sermons, his truths might have been lost in drab lecture. But by weaving tales around weddings and winepresses, he could not only bring wisdom within reach of the unlearned, he could silence the self-righteous with simple truth.

Take, for example, this story about the kind of clothes that should be worn to weddings.

Jesus told of a wedding garment so splendid, God deemed it the only one worthy to be worn to the great banquet of the kingdom. This garment was called grace. Many tried to pass the gatekeepers of that banquet inappropriately dressed.

But they did not prevail.

What, though, of that great banquet still to come?

❖ Some will come dressed in the garments of self-esteem.

❖ Others will dress in glitzy garments of Christian showbiz.

❖ Some will wear camouflage to hide their confession.

❖ Many will wear the look-alike uniforms of conformity.

❖ Some will dress mod in the latest theological fad.

❖ Others will clad themselves in denominational heritage.

❖ Many will come dressed in the robes of serious philosophy.

❖ Still others will come dressed in the ultra-tolerant garments of broad-mindedness.

❖ Others will impress with the formal wear of reputation.

But those who are admitted to the marriage supper of the Lamb will be clad in new grace. This lovely outfit will not be a self-made garment. They did not pay for it, for it cannot be purchased. When they acquired the garment, in fact, they were utterly bereft of all pride. They came to Christ in

> Lay aside the tatters of self-respect, and put on the Lord Jesus Christ.

the tatters of their sinful life and were restored. Then they were dressed in the clean white garments of his justification. Now at last in his new kingdom, they find themselves fully cleansed by Christ, who has made them acceptable for all time.

Prayer

Lord, how much I love you. You took all my righteousness—which was as filthy rags—and clothed me in the bright new robes of God's acceptance. For this I fall on my knees before you and adore you for bending so low to redeem me.

For additional Bible reading: Galatians 2:20–21

*"He still had one to send, a beloved son. Finally
he sent him to them, saying, 'They will respect my son.'
But those tenant farmers said among themselves,
'This is the heir. Come, let's kill him, and the inheritance
will be ours!' So they seized him and killed him,
and threw him out of the vineyard. Therefore, what
will the owner of the vineyard do?" (Mark 12:6–9)*

One Son. One needy world. These were the two ingredients of the last, best, all-sufficient plan of God.

He had earlier tried the prophets, but people always rejected their summons to salvation. These seers and sages had stood for centuries on the shorelines of eternity, crying out to those who were perishing. They watched with sadness as the people rejected their messages and the nation perished.

Finally, God sent Jesus.

But those who had earlier martyred the prophets soon made a martyr of God's only begotten Son.

Jesus' death states the dilemma of God in Mark 12: "What

will the owner of the vineyard do?" The very question tenderly lifts the grace of God and places it on the balance pan opposite his demand for justice. Either in this life or the one to come, pardon must be applied or retribution will be the sentence.

Both grace and retribution have one thing in common: they come with the tears of God. God wept when Jesus died. He could not save both his only beloved Son *and* humankind, so he chose to save humankind and let his Son die. But God still weeps over all who perish.

Are you thankful that God is a real Person—one who weeps at lostness? Yes, even more than that, he wept at your lostness. Is not his loving Fatherhood the constant endorsement of your self-worth? He has wept. Christ has died. You are loved. Rejoice!

> Grace is unexplainable. We Are all walking miracles of mercy.

Each time you take the wafer or sip the wine of Communion, think on this: the bread and wine are there to call you to remember the price he paid. Each time you think of Easter, think on this: of all your sins, the most grievous is walking past Calvary without remorse, feeling no need to apologize for Good Friday.

You and I were not cheaply redeemed. Can we let a day go by without remembering the cost?

Prayer

Lord Jesus, I must not approach Easter with a gratitude grown old and routine. I am saved by your blood and your Father's tears. I must praise you for love like this.

For additional Bible reading: 1 Peter 1:18–21

"The stone that the builders rejected, this has become the cornerstone. Everyone who falls on that stone will be broken to pieces, and if it falls on anyone, it will grind him to powder!" Then the scribes and the chief priests looked for a way to get their hands on Him that very hour, because they knew He had told this parable against them. (Luke 20:17–19)

The stone that the builders rejected, this has become the cornerstone."

We cannot fully understand this passage in the context of modern architectural procedure. Today, builders lay cornerstones in great ceremony after the building is finished. Usually some empty place—a square receptacle—is left in a wall, where the cornerstone will finally be inserted with great pomp. The cornerstone represents a time of finishing, a time for speech-making, a time of corporate celebration.

When Jesus spoke this parable, though, the cornerstone was understood to be the first stone laid on the foundation. Every measurement as to distance or rectitude was taken from the placement of that stone. The full weight of the growing building always fell on it. This stone both certified and created the building. Without it, the building was not possible. Jesus' listeners would have understood this.

In bringing up this ancient Scripture, Jesus was reminding the temple officials that the Messiah was to be the standard, the support, the creator of the faith. This promised one was not merely the object of theological dialogue; indeed, he was the faith itself.

This parable must have bitten into the self-righteous people with intense conviction. How they needed to hear him and embrace him as the center of their heritage. Alas, they did not. They rejected him whom God had sent to be their Redeemer.

Let us turn from the failure of these ancient theologians and ask ourselves what this defining text means to us:

❖ Do we build our own lives on this unfailing cornerstone?

Monolith of hope, stone of heaven's sovereignty, Gibraltar of the eons, rock of ages cleft for me.

❖ Is he foundational in all we choose to be and do?

❖ Do we measure the righteousness—the rectitude—of our own lives by his requirements?

❖ Is Jesus central to your life as the cornerstone, or is he only one philosophy among others?

If he is only one among equals for you, he will at last be a rock of offense—the stone that you as a builder have rejected, the stone that causes God to reject you.

Prayer

Lord, be the foundation stone for my life. May the solid granite of your purpose be the strong basis of my every dream. May I raise the superstructure of my life on your truth and faithfulness.

For additional Bible reading: Psalm 118:22–29

29 Days Until Easter

"O Jerusalem! Jerusalem that kills the prophets and stones those who are sent to her! How often I wanted to gather your children together, as a hen gathers her chicks under her wings, yet you were not willing! See! Your house is left to you desolate. For I tell you, you will never see Me again until you say, 'Blessed is He who comes in the name of the Lord!'" (Matthew 23:37–39)

A desperate protectionism rules throughout the world. It is called motherhood. Mothers have an unquenchable longing to protect and defend and keep their little ones safe.

Jesus capitalized on this drive to explain God's passion to redeem Jerusalem. God, like a mother hen, loved the world because it is his nature to love and protect.

In spite of all that mothers feel for their little ones, however, their little ones still maintain a will of their own. Each of us knows children raised in a loving home who chose to become stubborn, rebellious, and even criminal. All the time, the yearning instincts of their mother reached out to them to save and to love.

God is the lover of all the world at once. When Jesus offered this lament over Jerusalem, the world population was only scores of millions. Now there are more than six billion people in the world. Yet even in a world of billions, this amazing God reaches out in love to one person at a time. This is the raging testament of his singular grace. For in truth the world wants no other kind of love except that which comes one at a time.

Yet in spite of such love, the world still rejects Christ.

How Jesus wept at being rejected by his people. This rejection is not just a Jewish problem. Christ, like a mother hen, weeps over the entire lost and fragmented world. Alas, many of its inhabitants are still hard of heart—unwilling to be drawn.

> We are nothing more than confessing rebels, made loyal by Christ's great love.

So Christ still looks upon the modern cities of the world and declares, "Oh, Jerusalem—Oh, Chicago—Oh, Tokyo—Oh, London—how often I would have gathered you unto me as a hen gathers her chicks, but you were unwilling."

Prayer

Lord, help me to feel the yearning in your heart to love the city where I live. Help me to be more aware than ever this Easter season that you have placed me at my street address, my office cube, or my classroom to share the light of your love and grace in every corner of my world. In which of these subsets and suburbs shall I start to be used by you, to draw my city to yourself?

For additional Bible reading: 2 Peter 3:3–9

28 Days Until Easter

He came to Simon Peter, who asked Him, "Lord,
are You going to wash my feet?" Jesus answered him,
"What I'm doing you don't understand now, but afterward
you will know." "You will never wash my feet—ever!"
Peter said. Jesus replied, "If I don't wash you,
you have no part with Me." (John 13:6–8)

On this night before his death, Jesus assumed the position of a slave by washing his disciples' feet. Heaven's grand Lord stooped to serve his subjects. Jesus wrecked social custom to serve his bewildered disciples. The slave appointed for this kind of service was either off-duty or had been dismissed for the evening. So Jesus took up the slave's business, picked up a basin and towel . . . and amazed his men with a shocking impropriety.

When Jesus came to Peter, the fisherman braced himself in protest. *What?! The King of kings playing slave to the dirty-footed souls of such ordinary human beings?* It was not humble royalty but divine lunacy, as Peter saw it.

Are we not much the same? From babyhood on we are constantly being taught to take care of ourselves. But this kind of self-sufficiency can quickly become the foundation of pride. Jesus reminded Peter that he could not be included in the grace of God unless he was willing to let God serve him.

But can we really let God be our servant? Don't answer too quickly! Our willingness to be served by the Son of God speaks directly to our willingness to allow him to save us. We cannot be saved unless we're willing to accept God the servant and welcome him into our neediness. Only then can we accept his salvation and cherish it.

So when Jesus said to Peter, "Accept my service," he was in reality saying, "In the kingdom of God are some things you cannot do for yourself. For instance, you cannot pay for your own sin. Unless you accept what I have done for you, I can never own you. Washing feet may carry some humiliation, but my voluntary humiliation is the power of my servanthood. My servanthood must therefore walk the path of humiliation, or I cannot cleanse you of your pride and self-righteousness."

> Surrender the smaller coins of pride, and the gold of heaven shall be yours.

Prayer

Lord, help me not to cower in pride before the humiliation of your cross. I beg you: wash my feet. I implore you: cleanse me that I may be clean. Take my sin upon you that I may have my part in your eternal kingdom.

For additional Bible reading: 1 Timothy 1:15–17

27 Days Until Easter

When Jesus had washed their feet and put on His robe, He reclined again and said to them, "Do you know what I have done for you? You call Me Teacher and Lord. This is well said, for I am. So if I, your Lord and Teacher, have washed your feet, you also ought to wash one another's feet. For I have given you an example that you also should do just as I have done for you." (John 13:12–15)

The roads in Jesus' time were unpaved and people wore sandals, covering their feet with the dust and grime of their journey. When it rained, the roads became impassable seas of mud. When it was dry, the dust mixed with sweat to coat their feet and lower legs. So the end of every journey called out for clean feet. But water was often in short supply in the high desert country around Jerusalem.

This "upper room" dining experience seems to have occurred in a very large and well-furnished house. Such houses often had slaves whose task it was to take care of foot washing. It was the holiday season of Passover, however, so the servant might have had the night off. In this servant-less situation, it seems that each of the disciples had considered his station in life and had arrived at the conclusion that he was somewhat above this demeaning task.

Then into the smugness of their pride Jesus came to leave the whole world an example of how each of us might become like him. We can only follow him if we are willing to take up his work of the towel and basin. But the servant is never better than his lord. When we confess *Jesus* as Lord, nothing can ever again be beneath our dignity.

Consider these Easter ironies:

❖ The most menial and lowly task was once performed by the Son of the highest.

❖ The Messiah of majesty could stoop to serve the muck and mess of our misery.

❖ The root of royal Jesse could quit being King long enough to play the slave.

Such examples of humility still come from those who understand that servanthood is the stooping mandate of Jesus. The

> Christianity did not arrive with a mace and throne but with a towel and basin.

towel and basin are the most suitable symbols of all who want to follow Christ, of all who would be like him.

Prayer

Lord, help me take up the towel and basin, never forgetting that I am the servant and you are the Master. Truly teach me that the servant is never greater than his Lord; neither is he that is sent greater than he that sent him. What can I do to serve one of your creation this Easter season . . . even today?

For additional Bible reading: 1 Peter 4:8–11

Then one of the Twelve—the man called Judas Iscariot—went to the chief priests and said, "What are you willing to give me if I hand Him over to you?" So they weighed out 30 pieces of silver for him. And from that time he started looking for a good opportunity to betray Him.
(Matthew 26:14–16)

Jesus' disciples betrayed their Lord in two very different ways: Peter's way and Judas's way.

Peter actually denied Jesus while hanging around a courtyard fire. He lingered near enough to the fire to be sure he could see what was happening to Jesus throughout the long ordeal of the Savior's night trial.

Peter must have sat there hopefully. Buried by the bewildering confusion of all that was happening, he tried to pray that Jesus might somehow miraculously get out of this whole thing. Peter didn't go to the courtyard for the express purpose of denying Christ. In fact, just the opposite was probably true. He may have been there because he hoped to stand for Jesus.

> Perhaps the greatest of all sins is not to take sin seriously.

When the time came for his stand, however, he found he lacked sufficient courage to do it.

The denial of Judas, on the other hand, was a much more intentional betrayal. Judas sold Jesus in a conspiracy of plotting and conniving. But before we get too hard on Judas, let us ask: how much is Jesus worth to you? Most people who rail on Judas for betraying Jesus for thirty pieces of silver have often sold him out for much less. Perhaps the difference lies in how we sell Jesus. If in a moment of white-hot anger you betray Christ—as Peter did—in an unholy use of his name, you are less at fault than if you betray him as Judas did . . . in a premeditated way. The businessman who is lured incidentally into larceny may be easier forgiven than he who schemes his crimes.

All sin is sin, whether of Peter's sort or Judas's. But those premeditated sins that live in our hearts can canker and destroy a lifetime of relationships. James describes the worst effects of premeditated sins: "Each person is tempted when he is drawn away and enticed by his own evil desires. Then after desire has conceived, it gives birth to sin, and when sin is fully grown, it gives birth to death" (James 1:14–15).

We must never give evil a foothold in our conscience. Judas permitted evil into his heart and ended life with a jangling in his soul that overcame the jingle in his purse.

Prayer

Lord, I know I will never be able to call the sin in my life to a halt. But forgive me when I sit down to play chess with the devil. Cleanse my heart so that any premeditated evil will never find a welcome there.

For additional Bible reading: Psalm 19:12–14

25 Days Until Easter

When they were reclining and eating, Jesus said, "I assure you: One of you will betray Me—one who is eating with Me!" They began to be distressed and to say to Him one by one, "Surely not I?" He said to them, "It is one of the Twelve—the one who is dipping bread with Me in the bowl." (Mark 14:18–20)

It is always difficult to believe that our best friends are capable of proving themselves treacherous. Which of us has not from time to time suffered betrayal?

Treason is a terrible dream that haunts us all. Consider this dream: In this nightmare we find ourselves alone in a valley of twisted trees and dark forms, being pursued by a night stalker. We hurry through the shadowy forest. Close behind us, we can feel the hot breath of our demon assailant.

On we flee. The home of our best friend lies only a little way ahead; we can already see the lights through the rain-slick forest. Even harder we run. Suddenly we are out of the trees, and the house we call our security is just ahead. We quickly

> The words *friend* and *fiend* are separated by only a single letter.

approach the house and frantically knock. No one comes to the door. We knock again; now the stalker is close and almost there. We knock one last time. Our best friend in all the world—the one who might have saved us—is not at home.

There is no recourse. None can help, and the monster is upon us. All alone we turn to face the fiend. Lo! All the world is false! We face the night stalker only to discover it is the very face of the friend to whose house we had fled for hope. Treachery is the very fiend that terrorizes our need.

What can Judas have been thinking? Jesus was going to be arrested and crucified anyway. Judas could see that all the Jewish officials were angry with Jesus, and many wanted to put him to death. So Judas played the devil's servant. "*Et tu,* Judas? How can you? Judas—you with whom Jesus has eaten! Judas—you with whom Jesus has shared his company, his table, and his pilgrimage for three years!"

This was Jesus' greatest night of need. He would be dying tomorrow. He needed to be able to count on his friends. Alas, when he turned to these twelve who had pledged to save and protect him, it was Judas's face that was fanged. He whom Jesus had loved and called to special service had become the kissing killer of Gethsemane.

Could it be that any of us who would dip our hand into the bowl with Jesus might later plant the betrayer's kiss on his face in the garden?

Prayer

Lord Jesus, I am yours, but then so was Judas. I am known by all my friends to be your friend, but then so was Judas. I have usually done my Christian duty well, but then so did Judas. Help me to live in such utter honesty and devotion, I could never prove false in any Gethsemane.

For additional Bible reading: Hebrews 3:7–14

24 Days Until Easter

One of His disciples, whom Jesus loved, was reclining close beside Jesus. Simon Peter motioned to him to find out who it was He was talking about. So he leaned back against Jesus and asked Him, "Lord, who is it?" Jesus replied, "He's the one I give the piece of bread to after I have dipped it." When he had dipped the bread, He gave it to Judas, Simon Iscariot's son. (John 13:23–26)

The gauntlet was down. Jesus handed the morsel to Judas.

But notice! The Scriptures tell us oddly and, it seems, incidentally that Judas's father was Simon Iscariot.

Recently, a terrorist responsible for killing nearly two hundred innocent people was sentenced to death for his horrible crime. Once his sentence had been made public, his brokenhearted parents were interviewed. They were weeping and pleading with the judge to be lenient and not give the death penalty. They wept and reminded the press that "their son had always been a good boy." It was not until I saw their tear-stained faces that I was prone to remember that even terrorists have parents.

So, although we do not generally remember this, Judas had a father named Simon. He might have been dead by the time Good Friday occurred, but what if he was not? What if he was still alive that fatal Passover weekend? Did he weep to think what a horrible part his son was playing in the crucifixion of an innocent man? Judas complicated his treachery by committing suicide. Can these two horrible events, folding over on one another as they did, not have sent his father Simon into an impossible season of sorrow?

Of course, we cannot really know how the elder Iscariot dealt with all of this. Jesus counseled us also to reach out to the hurting. I believe that Jesus must have reached out to Judas. If he had the chance, he may have also reached out to his parents. Joy was about to be born on Resurrection morning, but Judas would already be dead. He would never taste that Easter joy. The grief of all those friends who would have helped him from time to time to repair his life could never find a place to do so.

Only he is God who loves when loving's out of fashion.

Remember that Jesus, three years earlier in the Nazarene synagogue, said that he had come to comfort the mourning. Let us watch for those all around us whose children live and die in disgrace and who wait for our comfort. Performing this kind of compassionate service could be your living legacy this very Easter. Be alert. The world is crying, and you hold the Kleenex.

Prayer

Lord, you came to comfort those who have had to live with shattering disappointments. We cannot fix all circumstance or dry all tears. But not to care is a great sin. Open my eyes to those around me who are in need of your tender love . . . and could perhaps feel it in my caring embrace.

For additional Bible reading: James 2:8–13

23 Days Until Easter

After Judas ate the piece of bread, Satan entered him. Therefore Jesus told him, "What you're doing, do quickly." None of those reclining at the table knew why He told him this. Since Judas kept the money-bag, some thought that Jesus was telling him, "Buy what we need for the festival," or that he should give something to the poor. After receiving the piece of bread, he went out immediately. And it was night. (John 13:27–30)

If you had a friend whom you knew was about to betray you, would you say to him, "What you're doing, do quickly," or would you cry out, "Stop that man any way you can"?

One thing I most admire about Jesus is that he was able to see the big purposes of God in the seemingly little things that were occurring. He knew it was God's will for him to die. During the last, few fleeting hours of his life, he could see that what Judas was doing was part of an unfolding, cosmic drama.

Herein lies the greatness of Jesus. He put the little pieces of life together as if he were assembling the flagstone walkway down which he would shortly walk. Stone by stone, he laid his own way into the center of the will of God.

So this is why he did not say, "Stop that man; he's going to betray me!" He saw that Judas's treachery, while not admirable, was just another stone in the pavement of the Via Dolorosa.

Jesus held in his mind a set of blueprints for human redemption. He was a carpenter and was probably used to reading building plans. He had taken these plans out of the inner sanctum of his heart and studied them in the wilderness, in private prayer. Throughout his long ministry he examined and reexamined these plans.

In Gethsemane he studied them yet again. There in the clear light of all he was asked to do, he said to the Father: "God, I find your plan heavy to be borne. Let this cup pass from me. But if I must drink the cup, let me drink it to the dregs. I find your plans heavy, but if I must bear them, strengthen me to carry everything."

> Gethsemane improves the visibility of things unseen.

Nothing mattered to Jesus but the pleasure of his Father. He mostly ached that Judas had stood next to divine love for three years and still chose to die beyond God's care.

How are you at assembling little things? How are you at taking little betrayals and great hurts and seeing the purposes of God in them? You will be like Jesus when you are willing to assemble your own pilgrimage from the flagstones of your pain.

Prayer

Lord, I believe that all things really are working together for good to those who love you. Still, I must remember that the ostracism of my friends plays its part in your great plan for my life. When I must endure such betrayal in order to be true to your calling, may I do it with an eye turned away from my own comfort and self-esteem—with an eye turned only toward the goal of eternity.

For additional Bible reading: Psalm 56:1–13

22 Days Until Easter

As they were eating, He took bread, blessed and broke it, gave it to them, and said, "Take it; this is My body." Then He took a cup, and after giving thanks, He gave it to them, and so they all drank from it. He said to them, "This is My blood of the new covenant, which is shed for many." (Mark 14:22–24)

Bread and wine: these are our sensate connections to our crucified Lord.

Jesus waits in heaven to return for us. In his absence his mystery remains very real. Though we cannot touch him with any of our five senses, he has left us a little photograph that we can pick up from time to time to contemplate his reality until he comes again.

What is this photograph of the senses that we can see, touch, smell, taste, and, yes, even hear? The bread and wine! We can hear the loaf tear and snap. We can behold the wine pouring into the chalice. We can taste it, smell it, and touch it. So our dull feelings come alive as we let our senses play with these wondrous elements that comprise our photograph of Calvary.

Did not Jesus know this on the night he took bread and blessed it? Did he not know that we needed to see the purple foam on top of the wine to see again from time to time the torment of Calvary? Did he not know that when we encounter mystery, we need a bit of affirmation from our five senses?

In handling what can be handled, then, we see a beautiful and redeeming picture of those things that *cannot* be handled—and we remember that the things which are most real are never the things that *can* be handled.

It is true that our redemption, as well as God's love, even heaven itself cannot be measured or studied. Yet these are the most real things there are. Jesus wanted us to handle the bread and wine—such temporary things—that by touching them we could think about what is truly real.

So the next time you're at communion . . .

❖ Study the church where the ritual is offered. It will pass away.

❖ Study the steel of the chalice and plate. They, too, are transient.

> Come feast and dine on bread and wine, and see the face of love.

❖ The pews you sit on are going to be gone some day.

The most real thing at the communion service is the piece of bread and the cup of wine. These remind us of that which is glorious and eternal. Its reality is more enduring than any of our five senses; it is hidden in our hearts—a photograph of all we own until we are in eternity with Christ.

Prayer

Lord, help me never to eat the loaf or drink the cup and not think of you. To hold the bread and wine is to celebrate all that I own that is of any real value.

For additional Bible reading: Hebrews 10:1–10

21 Days Until Easter

I assure you: I will no longer drink of the fruit of the vine until that day when I drink it new in the kingdom of God." After singing psalms, they went out to the Mount of Olives. (Mark 14:25–26)

The ritual of the Lord's Supper—the glass of wine—in time became a symbol of Christ's second coming. The apostle Paul wrote that each time we observe this rite, we do "proclaim the Lord's death until He comes" (1 Corinthians 11:26). In founding the observance, Jesus made it clear that this would not be the last glass of wine he would ever drink, but it would be the last he drank within the strictures of calendar time. His next glass would be savored in eternity.

The kingdom of God is one united continuum throughout eternity. Still, it definitely has two phases: present and future.

The kingdom of God that we enjoy in the present is God's kingdom in process.

The kingdom we will *one day* know is his future, completed kingdom. This finished kingdom we inherit will be that elevated state of existence we longed for while we lived on earth.

Each glass of remembrance is therefore a celebration of Christ's promise. A better kind of existence than mere physical life is on the way. We cannot know all that it will be, but we have Jesus' word that it will be better than anything we have ever known.

❖ The final kingdom will have no death or dying. Therefore, there will be no grief or bereavement.

❖ The glorious state to which all the redeemed are headed will have no pain or sickness.

❖ Night will never mark the margins of any day.

❖ Isaiah's vision of the peaceable kingdom will at last be a reality. The lion and the lamb will snuggle into the same meadow.

How odd that a meal of wine and bread should let us see what lies ahead.

But the best thing about his future kingdom is that it will be for us a new state of spirituality. We who have only known our Savior at a distance will behold his glory face to face. We will fall down at his feet in the everlasting praise that comes from a new intimacy with God.

So when Jesus talked about drinking new wine in the kingdom, he was speaking of a renovated spirituality.

This wine that once symbolized his awful dying will at last symbolize our new intimacy with him. We will drink deeply and freely of a new kind of life . . . and of a new and heightened love.

Prayer

Lord, I thank you for your cup of promise, for it is a symbol of two truths. First, life is transient. There will come a time when we will have our last sip and eat our last meal. Second, I thank you that what we now call our death is illusory. Life is eternal, and love is stronger than death.

For additional Bible reading: Revelation 21:1–7

"Peace I leave with you. My peace I give to you. I do not give to you as the world gives. Your heart must not be troubled or fearful. You have heard Me tell you, 'I am going away and I am coming to you.' If you loved Me, you would have rejoiced that I am going to the Father, because the Father is greater than I. I have told you now before it all happens, so that when it does happen, you may believe." (John 14:27–29)

Peace is the imperishable constant Christ provides our agitated souls. It causes us to remember that nothing is so out-of-control that it is beyond God's control. The world is not perishing; the skies are not falling. The fetid waters of our oasis have been sweetened to a drink of life. Peace is not the result of being able to shut our ugly circumstances into a throw-away container. Peace is the ability to accept his finished work on the cross even as we live through our current circumstances.

The martyrs often had more peace than those emperors who sentenced them to death. They had peace because they knew that Caesar was in control of nothing—certainly not their destinies. Caesar could not take their lives from them because they had already given them away.

This is the classic meaning of Paul's advice to the Romans: "Consider yourselves dead to sin, but alive to God in Christ Jesus" (Romans 6:11). All he really meant by this is that dead men do not have a long profit-and-loss ledger. They can lose nothing of value, since nothing that can be held in the hand of a corpse has any value at all. Even their lives have little value, since their earthly lives can only be reckoned in fragile years. You simply cannot threaten dead men.

Would you like to learn a song of peace that can quiet the riot of your hassled existence? Then ask the faithful martyrs of old. Peace for them was not the absence of war. It was not even the absence of threats. Peace was a lifestyle they manufactured from a worldview Jesus gave to them. The world could not take it away from them, since the world had not given it to them.

> There is no turmoil sufficient to disturb the peace of Christ.

Do you know such peace? If not, maybe it's time to move out of the hassle and into Christ. Life can create a chaos that steals your peace, but Christ can create in you a relationship that is all-consuming in its power. You will have peace—not because you grit your teeth to strain against your woes, but because in him no other way of life will occur to you.

Prayer

Lord, I know that I cannot have peace by merely craving it. Peace is nothing more than the by-product of wanting you. To want you is to have both you and peace without asking for either. Lord Jesus, I know that you possessed this peace, even as you prepared for death. May I too possess this gift of yours, even as I prepare for the next twenty-four hours—one single day of my life.

For additional Bible reading: Micah 5:1–5a

19 Days Until Easter

---

*"Look: An hour is coming, and has come, when you will
be scattered each to his own home, and you will leave Me
alone. Yet I am not alone, because the Father is with Me.
I have told you these things so that in Me you may have
peace. In the world you have suffering. But take courage!
I have conquered the world." (John 16:32–33)*

Are you beaten? Are you ready to throw in the towel? Has
discouragement wrapped its cold, gray fingers around your
heart, choking all your optimism? Beaten . . . beaten . . . beaten! What an odd word for believers to succumb to! Why
should any believer ever agree to let such a sour adjective define
a state of grace?

You have one way to take all the worries out of suspense novels:
read the last chapter before you begin the book. If the pictures
of universal judgment in Matthew 24 stood without hope, the
firestorms of final tribulation might seem too much to bear. But
when we see the white rider in Revelation 19, we can rejoice
ahead of time. Here we see the grandeur of the coming, reigning

Christ. And on his robe and on his thigh he has this name written: "King of kings and Lord of lords" (verse 16).

Jesus is the Overcomer with a capital "O," and we are the overcomers with a little "o." "In the world you have suffering" would seem a grand threat if the last part of the sentence were not this: "But take courage! I have conquered the world."

Think of what confident living would have come to Wellington before Waterloo if he could have had someone say, "General Wellington, here! I give you this picture of hope: Napoleon Bonaparte will surrender his sword to you tomorrow."

Or think how confident Eisenhower would have been in 1943 if someone had said to him, "Here is a photo to be taken two years from now—in 1945. See, sir, you are already the victor! Do not fret yourself over the outcome of this great world conflict. You are the designated winner. All you have to do is to live through the coming seasons. Discipline yourself for the conflict, but do not worry. The victory is yours."

Are you discouraged? Do you see no way to win the conflict? Has life dumped upon you more than you can

> To hold God's checkbook and die in poverty is to sin against his love.

bear? Then hurry to some quiet place. Read again that final chapter. Lift up your anthem of praise. Christ has overcome the world!

Prayer

Lord, I thank you for the photo of the grand finish you have already provided. As far as you are concerned, the race is past. I am the victor, and your conquest has guaranteed my security. Even as I look toward your cross in the coming days, may I see beyond it to your empty tomb . . . and know that what you have done in defeating death, you will also do through me. Hallelujah!

For additional Bible reading: 1 John 5:1–5

"I have glorified You on the earth by completing the work You gave Me to do. Now, Father, glorify Me in Your presence with that glory I had with You before the world existed. I have revealed Your name to the men You gave Me from the world. They were Yours, You gave them to Me, and they have kept Your word." (John 17:4–6)

Jesus celebrated his victory even before he began his decisive battle. He gloried in all that he would shortly finish—all that God had called him to do. The dying still lay ahead of him, but the purpose of his life was all but finished.

Learn this comforting lesson from him. Our confidence comes in knowing that we shall complete the tasks God has given us. Our trophy will be the inner reward which transforms our dying time into a celebration time.

The apostle Paul experienced an interesting metamorphosis in his view of death. In 1 Thessalonians he seems not to believe that he *will* die. He encouraged the church to remember that those who had already died before Jesus returned would be the first to be raised in the Second Coming. Then referring to his own future expectation, he continued, "We who are still alive at the Lord's coming will certainly have no advantage over those who have fallen asleep" (4:15).

Consider, however, his view in 2 Timothy, written at a much later date: "I am already being poured out as a drink offering, and the time for my departure is close. I have fought the good fight, I have finished the race, I have kept the faith" (4:6–7). Here the apostle is saying that he is ready to receive the reward of his labor: "the crown of righteousness, which the Lord, the righteous Judge, will give me on that day, and not only to me, but to all who have loved His appearing" (4:8). Having finished the race is Paul's way of saying what Jesus said: "I have completed the work you gave me to do."

The great burden of every follower of Christ is to come to know what God has called us to do in this world. Knowing this, we will have the unspeakable joy of anticipating how we will feel once we have done it.

> Living in eternal light is our final step after years of plodding forward in light less certain.

Dying knows a double blessing. The first blessing comes in possessing the security that when we close our eyes in death we will open them in heaven. The second blessing is the knowledge of having lived out our calling—by giving our lives to finishing the tasks he gave us to do.

Prayer

Lord, your blessed Holy Spirit has taught me my calling. Now that I am in the world, for as long as I am in the world, I will seek to complete all that you have given me to do. How glorious must be your final "well done" to those who knew what you wanted done, and therefore never lacked purpose in their living.

For additional Bible reading: Acts 20:22–24

17 Days Until Easter

Jesus said to them, "All of you will fall, because it is writ-ten: 'I will strike the shepherd, and the sheep will be scat-tered.' But after I have been resurrected, I will go ahead of you to Galilee." Peter told Him, "Even if everyone falls, yet I will not!" "I assure you," Jesus said to him, "today, this very night, before the rooster crows twice, you will deny Me three times!" (Mark 14:27–30)

Promises! Promises! How easy they are to make; how hard to keep! A famous poet once confessed that he had miles to go before he could sleep . . . and many promises to keep.

You already know the outcome of Peter's broken promises. But do not bludgeon the apostle for his weaknesses until you ask yourself, "Have I ever broken a promise to God?"

One that might quickly surface in your mind would be the promise you made to him when you were saved. All of us, in the process of salvation, promise Jesus that he can have our lives forever.

❖ You once promised him yours, remember? Have you broken that promise?

❖ You promised him your lips would always bear witness to his saving life. Have they?

❖ You promised him that your time would be his to do with as he pleased. Have you always given him such sway over your daily calendar?

❖ You promised him the faithful stewardship of your money. Have you been as generous as you said you would?

❖ You promised him your heart would not hold within it any image of moral compromise. Has your heart remained true to this?

Now that you remember your own weakness, go back and read Peter's promise. Yes, he would shortly break it, but his promise was made in the warmth of Jesus' fellowship. He broke it when he was separated from Christ and felt the glare of public accusations. This is nearly always the case. We make promises in the certain sunlight and break them in an unsure darkness.

What of your promises to honor Christ? Didn't you make them in the warmth of some special church service, or perhaps in

> Great victories for God are usually won in small, courageous battles.

the desperate gravity of a deep, personal trial? Did you break them in the pressure cooker of the secular world where the name of Christ held no reverence?

You, too, have miles to go before you sleep . . . and at least one grand promise you must keep. Will you?

Prayer

Lord, I promised you my life in the sunlight of old opportunities. Now here I am in the dark places, where promises made have lost some of their nerve and strength. How much I need you to help me keep these promises in place . . . in this place . . . at this time.

For additional Bible reading: Hebrews 10:35–39

16 Days Until Easter

Taking along Peter and the two sons of Zebedee, He began to be sorrowful and deeply distressed. Then He said to them, "My soul is swallowed up in sorrow—to the point of death. Remain here and stay awake with Me." Going a little farther, He fell on His face, praying, "My Father! If it is possible, let this cup pass from Me. Yet not as I will, but as You will." (Matthew 26:37–39)

Sometimes doing the difficult is possible only when we understand that God requires it.

Jesus had a cup to drink. God had required it. But merely lifting the cup to his lips was going to require every last ounce of two different kinds of endurance.

The first all-consuming endurance was physical. His body, youthful and firm, would be stretched between heaven and earth. He would hang by his hands in suffocating agony. Worse, he would not even be placed on the gallows until he had been physically abused and beaten. His head would be savagely wounded with a cruel crown of thorns. Jesus knew his blood would flow; his agony would be all but unbearable.

Yet the endurance perhaps even harder to bear was spiritual. He must live through the spiritual alienation he would feel when all his friends had rejected him, forcing him to die alone. He must then bear the sin of the world. He must experience that one awful moment when his Father turned his face away from the humanity-smudged holiness of his own Son. He must die in the realization that he would be dead forever if his Father did not raise him to life.

> "Thy will be done" is love's noblest proverb.

Naturally, he turned from the cup. What handsome and competent young rabbi in the prime of life would relish dying at thirty-three years of age? But Jesus despised one thing even more than drinking the hellish cup of crucifixion: what he really despised was disappointing his heavenly Father.

When the cup comes that you must drink, will you be obedient? Or will you seek to save your own reputation? Remember, Jesus didn't have a positive reputation on Good Friday. He sacrificed even that to please God.

Never love yourself more than you love serving the will of your Father in heaven. Sometimes his requirements can make

Gethsemanes out of ordinary gardens and Maundy Thursdays out of confident pleasures.

Prayer

Lord, give me whatever cup will honor you. Mingle it with bitterness and gall, if you must. But promise me that in my drinking of it, you will have the glory. Then gladly I will drink it all.

For additional Bible reading: 2 Corinthians 6:3–10

15 Days Until Easter

While [Jesus] was still speaking, Judas, one of the Twelve, suddenly arrived. With him was a mob, with swords and clubs, from the chief priests, the scribes, and the elders. His betrayer had given them a signal. "The one I kiss," he said, "He's the one; arrest Him and get Him securely away." So when he came, he went right up to Him and said, "Rabbi!"—and kissed Him. (Mark 14:43–45)

Betrayal and hypocrisy often dance together. Don't we see them intertwined in Judas—betraying Jesus while pretending to be his dearest friend at the same time?

The kiss of Judas! Long the theme of poetry and art! Long the arch symbol of treachery! Our fascination is not with the kiss. We are fascinated as to how Judas felt about what he did.

On the night of Christ's betrayal, Judas arrived in Gethsemane and kissed the Savior. This was nothing that the other disciples would have thought unusual. Kissing was the way people in ancient times greeted each other. But what the kiss said was that the person being kissed and the person doing the kissing were great friends. It was a loving gesture, an expression of warmth and familiarity.

Truly, the ones who are most guilty of keeping the church in splints and bandages are not usually the out-and-out enemies of Christianity. More often it is done by the pretended friends of Christ—those who project one kind of loyalty yet demonstrate another. The Judas kiss is a strong issue of duplicity that asks us to offer up our own definitions of testimony and loyalty. Sometimes we may actually give the impression that we don't know Jesus at all. Or we may be caught at some activity which others see. Then they wonder why our profession of faith and the living *out* of our faith dwell so far apart from each other.

> Live in such genuine simplicity that who you are is who you seem to be.

The only way to be of much use to God is to be sure that the image we project and the one we live out are the same. In our Gethsemanes we ought to be found as lovers of Christ.

Then hypocrisy and betrayal will not keep company in our lives.

Then what we profess to be and what we are will be the same thing.

Then the Jesus we name in public worship will also be the Jesus of our private worship.

Then our love will be as declarative in the darkness as it is in the light.

Prayer

Lord, did Judas kiss you with a blatant lie of open faithfulness? Help me to learn from his treachery. Help me take this bitter Easter moment deep into my heart, immunizing my loyalties from ever being able to declare my love while defying your right to rule over me. Keep me honest in the ministry I offer you.

For additional Bible reading: Proverbs 3:1–4

14 Days Until Easter

When they had lit a fire in the middle of the courtyard and sat down together, Peter sat among them. When a servant saw him sitting in the firelight, and looked closely at him, she said, "This man was with Him too." But he denied it: "Woman, I don't know Him!" After a little while, someone else saw him and said, "You're one of them too!" "Man, I am not!" Peter said . . . "I don't know what you're talking about!" Immediately, while he was still speaking, a rooster crowed. (Luke 22:55–58, 60)

Throughout the coming days, our focus will be on the most notable, most gripping events of the Holy Week. Again, we'll be contemplating these happenings so that we can live with them longer than a half-hour or two at a Good Friday service— so that we can awake on Easter morning with a surer sense of our salvation, with a deeper awe at the glory of resurrection.

So . . . come, let us wander into a torchlit courtyard in Jerusalem, abuzz with all the electric intensity of a developing news story: Jesus is on trial. His unorthodox chickens were coming home to roost (so the Pharisees thought). He is lined up in the crosshairs of mob justice. His disciples are scurrying into the shadows . . . to see without being seen.

Peter is among these lurking stragglers—a victim of his own weak commitment. Once, twice, three times he denies having anything to do with Jesus. Then he runs. He falls to his knees.

He weeps.

But lo, these are good tears! Our best tears are a sign of strength and not weakness. When we reach into our hearts and see what our betrayals have cost Christ, we ought to weep. Such well-spent tears measure not our betrayal but our authenticity. We are never more real than when we weep for what we know is wrong at the center of our lives.

Fear can be a good counselor, welding our frightened selves to God's sufficiency.

We have only to contrast Peter's tears with Judas's suicide to see why godly sorrow redeems us, while self-pity only condemns us. There is not a great deal of difference between what Judas did and what Peter did. The difference lies in how they reacted to it. Judas only grieved over his loss of place in the kingdom; Peter knew how much he had hurt his Savior.

Do your tears flow because you feel bad about your self-image? Let them flow because you know that your sins have hurt the heart of God, who has called you to be faithful to his Son.

Prayer

Lord, help me never to see my sins as having so little consequence that they may be dismissed without tears. Help me to feel some bit of Calvary in my every offense.

For additional Bible reading: 1 John 1:6–9

13 Days Until Easter

"You are a king then?" Pilate asked. "You say that I'm a king," Jesus replied. "I was born for this, and I have come into the world for this: to testify to the truth. Everyone who is of the truth listens to My voice." "What is truth?" said Pilate. After he had said this, he went out to the Jews again and told them, "I find no grounds for charging Him." (John 18:37–38)

Which doctrine of Christ is most important? I would say the doctrine of his sinlessness.

Some would argue, "What about his resurrection? Surely that is more important than his sinlessness?" Of course, in many ways the Resurrection created Christianity. If the Resurrection created it, though, the sinlessness of Christ authenticated it. If Jesus arose from the dead but only as a sinning Savior, could he truly save? In what way could a sinner's resurrection liberate the rest of us who need to be set free from our sin? To help us, Jesus must first be our moral superior.

Humankind has always struggled with sin. Even though the Greek religions carved their gods and goddesses to be ideal—well formed in body, strident and tall, a picture of what humankind was supposed to be—their gods were capricious and indulgent. No wonder their religion did not live.

Jesus, however, was sinless. Even Pilate could see that this man was not a criminal deserving of death. After hearing the witnesses against Jesus, Pilate said, "I find no grounds for charging Him."

Pilate may not have believed Jesus was sinless, but in some way he seemed to sense that Jesus was morally superior to him. Pilate spoke more than he knew. There was literally no fault *at all* in Jesus. He was, indeed, a lamb without spot and without blemish. He was the sacrifice offered once and for all for our sins.

Almost every religion has some sense of sin and has devised some ritual of forgiveness—always to no avail. The writer of Hebrews admitted that the ancient blood-sacrifice system of the Jews was also ineffective, if the sinner's trust was merely

All death was shattered by the sheer force of one life as it was meant to be lived.

in the ceremony: "For it is impossible for the blood of bulls and goats to take away sins" (Hebrews 10:4). What can be done, then? The apostle Paul wrote that God made one "who did not know sin to be sin for us, so that we might become the righteousness of God in Him" (2 Corinthians 5:21).

Jesus truly is the no-fault Savior. Because he was the perfect Son of God, your imperfections are covered by his blood. You are forever free!

Prayer

Lord, have we forgotten that it was your perfect life which covered our imperfections? Have we forgotten that the blood of your perfect sacrifice healed our sin? Because I am so sinful, I treasure a Savior who was tempted in all points like I am and yet lived without sin. Because of your sacrifice, my own sin is now removed as far from me as the east is from the west.

For additional Bible reading: Hebrews 7:23–28

Then the governor's soldiers took Jesus into headquarters and gathered the whole company around Him. They stripped Him and dressed Him in a scarlet robe. They twisted a crown out of thorns, put it on His head, and placed a reed in His right hand. And they knelt down before Him and mocked Him: "Hail, King of the Jews!" Then they spit on Him, took the reed, and kept hitting Him on the head. (Matthew 27:27–30)

They stripped Him."

This interesting phrase describes the trial of Jesus.

Why did they strip him? Why this naked abuse? Perhaps because when the accused is naked and the accusers are clothed, shame and humiliation are most intense.

Solzhenitsyn was once interrogated naked before a Russian tribunal. He said it was very hard to reply to any question before one's clothed accusers. To be forced to reply naked is the most irrational of humiliations.

Humiliation! How rightly Francis de Sales reminds us that

we cannot gain the virtue of humility without humiliation. Considering all that Jesus has done for us, I am amazed that we are so reluctant to bear any sort of embarrassment for his name. We want to be humble without enduring a cross or any loss of self-respect.

Yet Jesus, who was longsuffering in his tolerance of human abuse, waited through the naked mockery. Even this humiliation could not keep him from holding on to his identity. No level of taunting or torture could force him to forget who he was—the Messiah of salvation for which he now stood trial. He knew that on the cross, he would endure the mockery of Satan that he might destroy it forever.

Jesus' shame dealt a death blow to all our pretensions.

In his nakedness, then, he really knew no shame . . . because shame comes from knowing you have done something wrong and therefore deserve the abuse.

Jesus knew this was not the case. He had done nothing wrong. Thus, the endurance of this humiliation pleased God.

Obedience always does.

Prayer

Lord, I am ashamed that in your lonely hours of persecution, the full weight of my sin fell upon you. It was my sin for which you were hated, mistreated, and abused. As I think of the pain and humiliation that followed you to the cross, may I desire more than ever to be pure. Help me see in your vivid example that there is a purity of life so real, it is incapable of shame.

For additional Bible reading: 1 Peter 2:20–25

11 Days Until Easter

Those who passed by were yelling insults at Him, shaking their heads, and saying, "Ha! The One who would demolish the sanctuary and build it in three days, save Yourself by coming down from the cross!" In the same way, the chief priests with the scribes were mocking Him to one another and saying, "He saved others; He cannot save Himself!"... Even those who were crucified with Him were taunting Him. (Mark 15:29–32)

Some men of faith, these chief priests! They needed to see some grand sign before they came to believe. But what is *faith* anyway? Is it not the mark of real faith to keep on believing when you have not the slightest reason to do so?

How illogical their challenge! Was not Jesus himself enduring his dark hours by means of his faith? Jesus did not play at faith the way the chief priests did. He did not say, "God, if you are really God, how about knocking these chief priests about, just to prove to them that you and I are related." No, Jesus died and somehow proved his faith not by coming *down* from the cross, but by *staying* on it. He knew that real faith cannot be confirmed by some showy spectacle, but by literally hanging on when things got tough.

This is ever the way. Crosses are not the places where faith is killed but where it is proven. Jesus went on believing that God loved him. That's precisely the reason he would not come down. If he had come down, he could not have finished the work God had given him to do.

How fortunate that Jesus did not come down from the cross. If he had been so self-willed, there would have been a stack of chief priests piled up in human obelisks of bad manners and selfish insults. The chief priests were right: if Jesus were going to save others, he could not save himself. Precisely by not saving himself, he could guarantee eternal life to the world.

The priests' accusations, then, became the greatest paradox of all time. There was a depth of wisdom in their insult—"He saved

> We were saved at the outrageous expense of a love that could not cease and would not abandon us.

others; He cannot save himself"—which even the mocking clerics who spoke it did not begin to realize.

Christ died that we might live.

By not saving himself, he could save us.

Prayer

Lord, I live because you chose to die. I am saved because you allowed yourself to be lost. Thank you, Lord Jesus, for not doing what the chief priests taunted you to do. Through your willingness to die on that long ago wondrous day, I was given hope.

For additional Bible reading: Hebrews 11:13–16

10 Days Until Easter

From noon until three in the afternoon, darkness came over the whole land. At about three in the afternoon, Jesus cried out with a loud voice, "Elí, Elí, lemá sabachtháni?" that is, "My God, My God, why have You forsaken Me?" (Matthew 27:45–46)

Christ's ordeal had stretched on hour after hour. He had been arrested, cuffed, beaten, stripped, mocked, and flogged. By this time his agony must have been at its apex. From this agony he cried out, "My God, My God, why have You forsaken me?"

Let his agonizing cry seem as bold as it really was—the plaintive sobbing of a child who did not know how much more abuse he could withstand. See, too, the response of his Father. From heaven his longing Father reached down toward his hurting son. Brokenness and pain caused the suffering Son to reach upward toward his Father. Thus, love united these reaching, broken lovers.

This cry from the cross illustrates the humanity of Christ, but so much more. If the human Jesus was hurting in the midst of all this pain, the divine Christ must have remembered all that being Emmanuel meant.

This pain-wracked cry comes from the twenty-second psalm. In happier times it had furnished Jesus with many wonderful moments of worship in the little synagogue at Nazareth.

❖ As a boy, this psalm was only worship liturgy. On the cross it became a part of Jesus' dying appeal to his Father.

❖ When the cantor had sung it in the Nazarene synagogue, it was reflection. On the cross it became a throbbing, insistent question from God's broken, bleeding Son: "Father, have you forsaken me?"

If you must have an answer to this ninth-hour question, the answer is "No." God never forsook Jesus, just as Jesus never forsook his Father. God does hate sin. When Jesus bore the sins of the ages, God felt a remoteness that led him not to look on his Son; but he was with Jesus at every moment of his dying.

Best of all, here is Jesus' promise in your hard times. He will "never leave you or forsake you" (Hebrews 13:5).

> **Christ's presence is his promise. He is always there, always strong, always Jesus.**

Is your own cross hard to bear? Is your dying an unspeakable agony? Go ahead and cry, "Elí, Elí, lemá sabachtháni?" God's answer to you is also a resounding "No."

Prayer

Lord, thank you for being there when life hurts. Just as you never forsook Jesus, I know you will not forsake me. Indeed, you cannot forsake me without making Hebrews 13:5 a lie, and you are the God who cannot lie.

For additional Bible reading: Deuteronomy 31:1–8

9 Days Until Easter

It was now about noon, and darkness came over the whole land until three, because the sun's light failed. The curtain of the sanctuary was split down the middle. And Jesus called out with a loud voice, "Father, 'into Your hands I entrust My spirit.'" Saying this, He breathed His last. (Luke 23:44–46)

Here are seven words you should reserve for your dying: "Into Your hands I entrust my spirit."

In our years of walking with Jesus, many of our steps must be taken in the dark, in times of great uncertainty. But the last step we experience is a step we need not fear to take. The last step will always be in the light. The dying time is the time for spending these seven words: "Into Your hands I entrust my spirit."

Perhaps you are young. Perhaps Jesus' final words do not seem to you to be anything you will need for many decades. Let this be your counsel: find an older friend and draw close to him. Make sure this older friend is a Christian. Then watch him live out his final years. If God should make it possible, watch this older believer change worlds.

You will see a grand confidence in him as he spends these final words. Best of all, you will see that only by watching people die is it often possible to find out what they really believe. Only from the end of life can we test those philosophies we said we believed during our younger years. Those who die well have lived well. Those who can say with peace and utter resolve, "Into Your hands I entrust my spirit," are those whose dying proves they lived well.

> # Dying was once thought to be the end of everything, but that was before Jesus died.

Only one confident end awaits all of us who are flesh. It is to be able to use Jesus' words legitimately, "Father, into Your hands." Those who can use these words understand why Jesus died. They have ascertained the confidence Jesus placed in his heavenly Father—the certainty he sensed when he closed his eyes for the final time.

This is the greatest part of the gospel. It is to publish Jesus' dying words as the hope of every heart. It is to give the final cross cry to every person.

Sooner or later, all must close their eyes for the last time. If in such a moment they possess the final words of the cross, they will be able to say clearly, "Earth is receding but heaven is approaching. This is my long-anticipated moment of oneness with the Father! Into your hands I entrust my spirit."

Prayer

Lord, I treasure your famous, final words. Help me to keep them handy when it is my turn to use them.

For additional Bible reading: Psalm 31:1–5

8 Days Until Easter

The next day, which followed the preparation day, the chief priests and the Pharisees gathered before Pilate and said, "Sir, we remember that while this deceiver was still alive, He said, 'After three days I will rise again.' Therefore give orders that the tomb be made secure until the third day. Otherwise, His disciples may come, steal Him, and tell the people, 'He has been raised from the dead.'" (Matthew 27:62–64)

Life seems to finish in one of two ways. Either we expect the exciting and unbelievable; or like Pilate's garrison, we watch graves, expecting nothing. These sentries expected nothing supernatural, so they sat up for three days and nights watching for grave robbers. Then when God blew the lid off the tomb, they were traumatized, as silent as dead men. Those who never expected Jesus to live again were shocked by the detonation of joy when he returned—and made all life possible.

In this world, people will either trust and find themselves gaping over the unbelievable things God brings their way, or they will doubt and stumble over the acts of the unbelievable God.

Those who doubt are forever confused that the great mysteries of God never blessed them but only stupefied them.

Unbelief sets guards over sealed tombs—guards who expect nothing. These rock-watchers—"the chief priests and the Pharisees"— wanted to make sure no one stole

"He is Risen!" is earth's ultimate surprise.

Jesus' body. They all claimed to love God and honor all of Judaism's promises of Messianism. Yet the Messiah's Easter life surprised them.

Can it be that men and women can love God with a level of passion yet really be ignorant of the awesome possibilities that live in tombs? Yes! Religion sometimes wears a smug and practiced religiosity that is without vitality, expecting nothing. Most churchmen have long ago given up the hope of ever seeing the living Christ. They have traded their lost expectations for the dull habit of guarding rocks.

Now let us come to Easter . . . where one rock turned out to be worth watching. This rock quaked and split. Then the Lord Jesus, with certain tread, marched out as Victor. The unsettling event left the soldiers at first quaking, then later lying about what they saw.

But those doubtful, frightened followers of Christ erupted in a dance of joy that continues to this very moment. "He is risen!" is an anthem that outlives both rocks and unbelieving people.

Let us, the believing, begin the dance of joy—the resurrection life has come!

Prayer

Lord, your resurrection shook the earth. Indeed, it is still shaking it. Even more importantly, it is still shaking my life. As I approach the final week before Easter, may I find myself a grateful recipient of your Calvary grace, but even more an awed worshiper at your empty tomb.

For additional Bible reading: Psalm 102:25–28

7 Days Until Easter

The angel told the women, "Don't be afraid, because I know you are looking for Jesus who was crucified. He is not here! For He has been resurrected, just as He said. Come and see the place where He lay. Then go quickly and tell His disciples, 'He has been raised from the dead. In fact, He is going ahead of you to Galilee; you will see Him there.' Listen, I have told you." (Matthew 28:5–7)

We would not remember Jonah at all if he had merely been swallowed by a fish. The only element of the story that makes it memorable was that the prophet came out of the fish. "Out of the fish" makes Jonah a tale never to be forgotten.

Jesus said Jonah was a reminder of an oft-revealed plan: "This generation is an evil generation. It demands a sign, but no sign will be given to it but the sign of Jonah. For just as Jonah became a sign to the people of Nineveh, so also the Son of Man will be to this generation" (Luke 11:29–30). "For as Jonah was in the belly of the great fish three days and three nights, so the Son of Man will be in the heart of the earth three days and three nights" (Matthew 12:40).

We would likewise not remember the story of Jesus if he had been put in the earth and swallowed whole by *rigor mortis* and decomposition. Certainly, the cross is central to our faith. But if Christ's life story had ended between two petty thieves on a dusty knoll, we would have no Easter joy.

We remember Jesus because the earth, like Jonah's bewildered fish, had to yield him up again. Now we will never forget the wonder of Jesus' story—dead, though not for long, then alive forever.

"He has been resurrected, just as He said," the angels announced. This reminds us that however the resurrection may have surprised the apostles, it did not surprise God. Here was a miracle so carefully orchestrated that Jesus had told his disciples long before he died that he would rise again (Matthew 16:21)—not just to make a splash by walking out of the tomb, but to give us all a wonderful new life, forever unstoppable.

He lives!
What marvelous
madness!
What glorious
insanity!

What the angels reported as a current event, we now accept as a part of holy history. But do we accept it so rationally, so histori-cally, that our matter-of-fact attitude toward it has stolen its vitality? May this never be so. May the living Christ daily bring to your life the joy that made Easter a world-changing truth. May this truth continue daily to change your attitude and charge your dreams.

Prayer

Lord, you live, and because of that, so do I. You will never die again, and because of that, I too will find death of no eternal consequence. Help me worship you today, not like those who rained fickle hosannas on you as you rode into Jerusalem on the back of a donkey, but with the submitted, surrendered heart of a true believer.

For additional Bible reading: Jonah 2:5–9

6 Days Until Easter

It was as [Jesus] reclined at the table with them that He took the bread, blessed and broke it, and gave it to them. Then their eyes were opened, and they recognized Him; but He disappeared from their sight. So they said to each other, "Weren't our hearts ablaze within us while He was talking with us on the road and explaining the Scriptures to us?" (Luke 24:30–32)

Emotion is not the evidence that a religion is true, but emotion is always the by-product of true religion. Why? Everything which impacts our lives at the deepest level of our souls cannot help but elicit our deepest, most profound feelings.

"Weren't our hearts ablaze within us?" confessed these two on the road to Emmaus. Yes, they "felt" the presence of Jesus. Why wouldn't they? Their weekend had been shattered to a thousand splintering shards of brokenness by the death of their dearest friend. Now, wondrously, he was alive again. He was present with them. They were there . . . with Jesus. How could they not help but experience emotion?

Can you not remember when you were first with Jesus?

❖ Did you not feel his presence burning within you?

❖ Was there not at first an outpouring of godly sorrow when you realized how much it required for Jesus to save you?

❖ Then were there not moments of quiet reflection when you were overwhelmed with the greatness of the Son of God?

❖ Was not this hush in your heart reluctant to speak lest there be a transgression against the holy silence in the center of your soul?

❖ Then at last, did not joy in wild exuberance wash over you like a mighty river? Was this joy not completely uncontrollable?

In short, you met Jesus! You felt all that these two felt on the road to Emmaus. Your heart burned within you as you felt the presence of Jesus.

It still burns within you, does it not, when you feel his nearness?

His scars are evidence that heaven knows no blood or pain.

Prayer

Lord, may I never be passive in your presence. May your nearness ever excite me. May songs and praises be the definitions of my deportment when I feel your nearness. In this blessed week of Easter, may I see your wounds, touch your face, sense your power . . . and feel my worship.

For additional Bible reading: Psalm 103:1–5

5 Days Until Easter

"Look at My hands and My feet, that it is I Myself! Touch Me and see, because a ghost does not have flesh and bones as you can see I have." Having said this, He showed them His hands and feet. But while they still were amazed and unbelieving because of their joy, He asked them, "Do you have anything here to eat?" So they gave Him a piece of a broiled fish, and He took it and ate in their presence.
(Luke 24:39–43)

In this incredible resurrection moment, Jesus asked for something to eat, because by eating he could fully convince his disciples that he was not a ghost. Later, according to the Gospel of John, he also ate breakfast with them beside the sea. (He even seems to be the one doing the cooking!) Since ghosts have no physical substance and would not eat solid food (and ghosts are certainly not substantial enough to cook breakfast), this quite ordinary request of Jesus blew away all notion that he was a poltergeist, a figment of their imagination, a phantom.

A heresy developed within the early church called *docetism* (based on the Greek word *dokeo*, "to seem"). This heresy taught that Jesus was not *really* a person but only looked like one. Some said that Jesus was a real person in *life*, but that after the Resurrection he was only an apparition.

The easiest way for Jesus to prove he wasn't a ghost was to ask for a piece of fish. This small morsel, eaten by the resurrected Christ, was proof to all of them that the Resurrection was real.

But the best way to prove that Jesus is still real is not to argue that he once ate solid food. The best argument for you and me today is that he is still touching and redeeming all life, beginning with our own.

> **Jesus has power enough to fashion thrones from cynic's hearts.**

I have never been able to doubt Christ for very long, because he will not leave me alone for very long. I am much like the philosopher who after trying to be an atheist gave up all hope. Why? He said that if we try to dismiss Christ as a man, he haunts us as an idea. If we try to dismiss him as an idea, he haunts us as a man.

I must confess that when I try to do without Jesus, my life is so empty and purposeless that I know I must hold him in my heart if life is ever to make sense again. I have seen him do many wonderful and beautiful things. Doubt him for very long, and we will find his reality where we have always found it—in our hearts.

Prayer

Lord, because of your living presence in my heart, may your reality go unquestioned among my friends. Help them to look at me and clearly see that you are the most real thing there is about me.

For additional Bible reading: Colossians 3:15–17

4 Days Until Easter

Jesus came, stood among them, and said to them, "Peace to you!" Having said this, He showed them His hands and His side. So the disciples rejoiced when they saw the Lord. Jesus said to them again, "Peace to you! Just as the Father has sent Me, I also send you." After saying this, He breathed on them and said, "Receive the Holy Spirit."
(John 20:19–22)

What a glorious trusteeship is ours. Jesus breathed on his disciples and imparted the Holy Spirit. This blessed Comforter was about to be fully born in power on the day of Pentecost. But as Jesus breathed on them, he gave them this assignment: "Just as the Father has sent me, I also send you."

Jesus' assignment from his Father is in some ways no different than our assignment from him. Jesus had come "to preach good news to the poor . . . to proclaim freedom to the captives and recovery of sight to the blind, to set free the oppressed, to proclaim the year of the Lord's favor" (Luke 4:18–19).

In this description of his calling, we hear the description of our own calling. Jesus boiled this assignment down to its root idea when he said, "The Son of Man has come to seek and to save the lost" (Luke 19:10).

Consider the glory of our assignment! We have been given the calling to help change the destiny of souls. As Jesus was sent, so are we.

The breath of Christ! How the church needs it, and yet how we turn from it. So often when we say or sing, "Holy Spirit, breathe on me," we really mean, "Let me taste and feel the power of your Holy Spirit, but don't make me to do anything that would embarrass me or take too much of my time."

> Do you long for the adventure of living in Christ's power? Stand still. Receive.

But to receive this glorious Christ is to allow him to breathe into us his wonderful empowerment. Once empowered, our joyous duty is to go into the world doing exactly what he did—seeking and saving those who are lost.

Who can live without this empowering breath?
Who would want to?

Prayer

Lord, for so many years I have approached Easter without ever see-ing past what your love on Calvary has done for me. Yet today you inspire me to look beyond my own forgiven sin and see those who are still putting their confidence in that which cannot save. Lord, send me to them, but not until you have breathed on me. I want to serve you, but not without your empowering spirit. It is not possible to do your work without your power.

For additional Bible reading: Romans 15:17–21

3 Days Until Easter

After eight days His disciples were indoors again, and Thomas was with them. Even though the doors were locked, Jesus came and stood among them. He said, "Peace to you!" Then He said to Thomas, "Put your finger here and observe My hands. Reach out your hand and put it into My side. Don't be an unbeliever, but a believer." Thomas responded to Him, "My Lord and my God!"
(John 20:26–28)

The faith of the practical and steady disciples provides the ballast for those who are always ecstatically eager to believe too soon. Thomas was not the kind of gullible soul who would buy the Sea of Galilee just because some carnival barker said it was for sale.

Thomas had been there the night we know as Maundy Thursday, when Jesus had shared the bread and the wine with his closest friends. He had either seen Jesus' death with his own eyes or heard enough back-alley reports to become convinced that his Master was truly dead. So he was not overly quick to believe the incredible tale of Christ's resurrection.

Still, Jesus helped Thomas to realize that only when we are ready to believe in the Resurrection can we be saved. Paul said much the same thing: "If you confess with your mouth, 'Jesus is Lord,' and believe in your heart that God raised Him from the dead, you will be saved" (Romans 10:9). This miracle is the centerpiece of the Christian faith. No one becomes a Christian by merely believing in Christ's teachings. Christianity is not the acceptance of a lot of "be-good" doctrine.

> Consider his scars and hear him say, "These I gained in loving You."

So Thomas believed. He cried, "My Lord and my God," to which Jesus responded, "Because you have seen Me, you have believed. Blessed are those who believe without seeing" (John 20:29).

Felix, to whom Paul made his legal appeal, came to the Resurrection and stumbled. All of those to whom Paul preached on Mars Hill seemed to be moving toward faith until Paul brought up the Resurrection. They committed Thomas's sin, clung to doubt, and were lost forever.

How honest Jesus was with Thomas. He would have been as lost as those on Mars Hill if he had never believed.

The greatest evidence of the living Christ in our day is that we, later in time, have been given the faith to see and believe. We know he lives—we know!—not only because he came out of the tomb on Easter morning, but because he lives within our hearts.

Prayer

Lord, I've received too much life from you to doubt that there is life in you. In this coming weekend of Easter remembrance, help me experience your life again, to believe what I cannot always see but which I know to be true: that you are "my Lord and my God."

For additional Bible reading: 1 Peter 1:8–13

2 Days Until Easter

Then Jesus came near and said to them, "All authority has been given to Me in heaven and on earth. Go, therefore, and make disciples of all nations, baptizing them in the name of the Father and of the Son and of the Holy Spirit, teaching them to observe everything I have commanded you. And remember, I am with you always, to the end of the age." (Matthew 28:18–20)

We come to Good Friday. We remember the cross. We hear the words of Christ, spoken without fear yet cried through impossible pain:

❖ "My God, my God, why have You forsaken Me?"

❖ "Father, forgive them, because they do not know what they are doing."

❖ "Into Your hands I entrust My spirit."

❖ "It is finished!"

Gripping words. Powerful words. But what were Jesus' *final* words? Here in the closing moments of his time on earth, the resurrected Lord spoke of taking his message to the world. There is no question what he considered most important.

What is undeniable is that he is telling all his followers their lives are global in their consequence. Here is the force of Christ, the master motivator, imparting a dream of ultimate significance. Thus he leaves his church. He ascends and is gone. There stand the motivees.

Are they afraid of this gigantic dream he has left them? Hardly! They know they are to wait in Jerusalem until the Spirit comes. So empowered, they will march in obedience to Christ's command. No use lamenting that they are people with no national reputation. No reason for protesting that they are not graduates of prestigious academies. They are in love with their commander, and he is in love with the lost world.

> Since you'll be going into all the world anyway, make disciples as you go.

Their assignment will not overwhelm them. Why? Because Christ has promised, "Remember, I am with you always, to the end of the age." Their task is great, but they do not have to accomplish it alone.

Is not this same task yours? Do you not also have the promise of Christ? Yes, he will be with you. The task ahead will never be overwhelming. Best of all, in the company of Christ, your life will never lack significance.

Prayer

Lord, the cross bears the marks of maturity on my soul this year. Through it I see the price of my salvation and the reason for me to forsake the sin that drove you there. But through it I also see a world so full of your lost lovers. I must never forget how much you love them. I must never walk by anyone who doesn't know you without wondering if you want to use me to make the introduction.

For additional Bible reading: 1 Kings 8:56–61

1 Day Until Easter

After He had said this, He was taken up as they were watching, and a cloud received Him out of their sight. While He was going, they were gazing into heaven, and suddenly two men in white clothes stood by them. They said, "Men of Galilee, why do you stand looking up into heaven? This Jesus, who has been taken from you into heaven, will come in the same way that you have seen Him going into heaven." (Acts 1:9–11)

This promise took the bereavement out of Jesus' leaving. "This is not 'good-bye!' This is 'see you later!'" said the angels. With this promise the church had a double blessing. They knew the Holy Spirit would soon arrive, and they had the certain promise that Jesus himself would come again in the same manner they had seen him go. With the ascension, Jesus' thirty-three years on earth were ended until such time as he would return to set up his millennial reign of peace.

Is there a bit of rebuke in the angels' question: "Why do you stand looking up into heaven?" So many across the past two

> Those too
> hurried to
> await his
> appearance
> will likely run
> past his power
> in the present.

thousand years have formed study groups to figure out the "when" of Jesus' second coming. They are fervently thumbing their prophecy books, plotting their time lines, scanning the skies watching for his return.

"That's such a pointless activity," said the angels. "Jesus will come as he went . . . when he's good and ready. In the meantime you have much work to be done."

Perhaps the words of the angels were enough to send the disciples scurrying back into the city, much as they had scattered on the Saturday following his death—only this time a famous ten-day prayer meeting was getting underway. At the end of that time, the Holy Spirit would descend in power. The wind and flame would empower the church for its conquest of a fallen world. From the very outset—by the thousands—they would be swept up into Christ until now billions of souls claim to be his followers.

How different the world might have been had not these early witnesses of the ascension obeyed the words, "Quit looking up into the sky!" In awe of the heavenly messenger, they indeed stopped looking.

Still, the courageous work of sharing God's love must find all believers sometimes taking a quick glance at the sky.

You just never know when he will come again.

Prayer

Lord, empower me. Even on this day before Easter, send me out into the world. Come whenever you want to. I will be most glad to see you.

For additional Bible reading: 1 Thessalonians 5:1–11

Easter Sunday

I, John, your brother and partner in the tribulation, king-dom, and perseverance in Jesus, was on the island called Patmos because of God's word and the testimony about Jesus. I was in the Spirit on the Lord's day, and I heard behind me a loud voice like a trumpet. . . . When I saw Him, I fell at His feet like a dead man. He laid His right hand on me, and said, "Don't be afraid! I am the First and the Last, and the Living One. I was dead, but look—I am alive forever and ever." (Revelation 1:9–10, 17–18)

There is a double-exposure photograph in the heart of every believer. One image is of the dying Christ, captive to human laws and small decrees, crying, "It is finished!" The other image is of the Christ of the Apocalypse, bursting through the skies, clothed in lightning, crying, "*History* is finished!"

He is coming in the clouds with power and great glory. How wonderful it will be to behold this great finale! This truth is the great "not yet" of the New Testament. All else written there is now biblical history. Not this! Jesus, who left Olivet in

ADs 30 or so, has yet to complete the prophecy the two angels gave as Jesus rose into heaven.

Anything finished holds little interest. If we could look back and see that Jesus had already finished up the faith in the first century, we might be prone to say, "Jesus was on earth once with James and John (ho hum), but that's all past now. It must have been nice back in the good old days when things were really popping."

> The wonder of Easter is as real and certain as sunrise. "He lives!" is the very definition of significance.

But Jesus is just as much our contemporary on this Easter day as he was the contemporary of Matthew, Mark, Luke, and John. In fact, we may get to see what his disciples only dreamed about. Jesus is not only risen; he is coming again! And we may get to see this cloud-splitting finale any day now—with our very own eyes!

What shall we do in the meantime? Shall we find ourselves crying, "We sure wish we could have seen Jesus when he came around the first time"? No, never! We indeed shall see him. Every eye shall see him! Then we who stand at the end of

Christianity will see that we were just as much participants in the life of Christ as those who knew him in the first century.

Happy Easter. He is risen indeed.

Come, Lord Jesus.

Prayer

Lord, I long to see you, to behold what all the ages have dreamed about. Come quickly! May we be among that great crowd who behold the risen Christ reigning over the church triumphant.

For additional Bible reading: Revelation 22:16–17